When Down Looks Up

One Mother's Journey from Personal Crisis to Divine Purpose

Karen E. Donahue

Foreword By: Andrea Procko, MS, PhD, LCGC

Written By: Karen Donahue
© 2020

ALL RIGHTS RESERVED. No part of this book may be reproduced in any written, electronic, recording, or photocopying without written permission of the publisher or author. The exception would be in the case of brief quotations embodied in the critical articles or reviews and pages where permission is specifically granted by the publisher or author.

LEGAL DISCLAIMER. Although the author and publisher have made every effort to ensure that the information in this book was correct at press time, the author and publisher do not assume and hereby disclaim any liability to any party for any loss, damage, or disruption caused by errors or omissions, whether such errors or omissions result from negligence, accident, or any other cause.

Publishing Service By: Pen Legacy®
Cover Picture: Ann Landstrom of Ann Photography

Library of Congress Cataloging – in- Publication Data has been applied for.
Paperback ISBN: 978-0-8600483-5-0
PRINTED IN THE UNITED STATES OF AMERICA.

~~~FOREWORD~~~

As genetic counselors, we are privileged to hear the stories of our patients and their families. Sometimes we play an important role in those stories – like being the one to give a new diagnosis. No two stories are ever the same, but each helps us to understand others a little more.

While working in the clinic one day, I had the good fortune of getting a phone call from Karen Donahue. She wanted to know how she could use her family's story and experiences to help other families who had received a Down syndrome diagnosis for their loved one. As we talked that Friday afternoon, her passion and love came through the phone line. It felt as if we had known each other for a long time and were sitting in the same room, chatting over a cup of coffee. During the time that we have been working together, Karen's dedication to improving her daughter's life and the lives of all children whose abilities are different has continued to come through as her mission and joy.

Karen and her family were not our patients, but as I've gotten to know her, she has looked for and embraced opportunities to share her story with my patients, colleagues, and students. Over the years, Karen has graciously integrated several of my students into her story. She welcomes them into her family life outside the clinic in a way that will stay with each of them forever and make them, as well as myself, a better asset to each new family who we are privileged to meet. I thank her for sharing her story with all of us.

Andrea Procko, MS, PhD, LCGC

Genetic Counselor

~~~ACKNOWLEDGEMENTS~~~
Much Gratitude, Dedication and Love to:

My children, *W, A, Kristina* and *L...forgiving my many flaws and missteps as your mother. YOU are ALL my Angels, Teachers & Sunshine on my cloudiest days!*

To Betty & Don Turner, *M & D...Saying yes to love and acceptance by fostering, mentoring me & welcoming me as a family member. I have never forgotten or taken for granted, your selflessness. You are loved*

Ann Photography*...you captured the most beautiful and sensitive essence of Kristina and myself during our photography session with you! Your talent lives forever!*

Barbara Hasty*...You, were the most influential music teacher I have ever known. Your compassion, commitment and determination inspired me to use my voice through song and in life. **You** made me feel as though I was worth saving!*

Terri Mullen Smith*...your story, your love for me all of these years, immeasurable!*

James B, *My first boyfriend! I will always remember, among other important things, your gift of love and support &, "I Am Woman"*

K.S.C.*, For loving me all of these years! You have been the most trusted, stable person I've ever had or needed in my life! "Yours Truly"*

St Madeline Sophie Center & Noah Homes

As **HEROS**, *you, your staff, continue to give people with Special Needs a fighting chance to be the best human they can be…with grace, dignity and respect for all you serve. May there be more programs like yours for people like my precious daughter Kristina A. Van Gelder*

To my **<u>Lord</u>** *and* **<u>Savior</u>****,** **<u>Jesus</u>** **<u>Christ</u>** *who "saved a wretch like me in 1972!*

~~~INTRODUCTION~~~

Early in 2019, a weekend evening spent with my daughter who was born with Down syndrome, inspired me to write this book. I had written the manuscript, but had not had it edited just yet. As 2019 ended and 2020 began, the unexpected and unimaginable happened for billions of people around the globe! The year started in the usual fashion, with a celebration on New Year's Eve. Afterward, we humans expected to go with the flow of life like most previous years. However, this *thing* called COVID-19 started a pandemic. Unbeknownst to many, this virus would be devastating to thousands of people.

When the year began, no one planned to experience something so life-altering that it would cause us to take a giant pause. Life was supposed to go on with its usual fanfare of us making plans for renewed goals, convictions, and plans to live better lives. For countless people, life stopped in its tracks – economically, socially, and for many, permanently due to an untimely death from this virus. No one really understood the magnitude of this pandemic and how quickly it would affect everything and everyone in all corners of the earth. Because of the widespread, deadly nature of this novel coronavirus, nearly everyone's future seemed to be forcibly placed on hold.

As if things weren't bad enough, our nation (and the world) witnessed people rioting in the streets over the unjust, untimely deaths of George Floyd, Breonna Taylor, Ahmaud Arbery and too many other souls of color. The pandemic exposed the burgeoning divide of social justice, racism, the wealthy and well connected compared to the less fortunate. To round out all of this chaos, it was an election year! Republicans and Democrats vilifying each other. Politicizing Covid-19 further pitting people against each other; those who were willing to listen to science, wear a mask, social distance for protection, and those who believe otherwise, thus refuse and refute it all. Deciding whether or not to vote by mail or risk catching the virus by showing up to the polls in person. The unfathomable fear people were already faced with, was furthered by the possibility the United States Postal Service who could or would somehow interfere with any citizen's vote for our country's next president seemed almost too much to bear.

I have had this book in mind for many years. Consequently, it seems I am either on time or my timing is way off by publishing this story at this time. My ultimate desire for writing it had a myriad of reasons behind it, including but not limited to raising awareness (and funds) for people with special needs. Too often, these innocent people are the last to be considered in financial policymaking and the first to be cut from said funding. Because of the current state of affairs around the world and America, it is very easy to push aside the present needs of those who have disabilities. Most are not able to advocate or speak for themselves. We need more passionate advocates in order to direct change for the better in Washington and beyond. Therefore, I feel this writing is timely and necessary for me to accomplish.

My daughter Kristina is one such person who needs an advocate. She is mostly nonverbal and unable to take care of herself. She is not living at home with me, but did so from birth until she was nineteen years of age. Currently, she resides in a residential community of ninety other people with special needs.

Towards the end of March of 2020, due to the dangerous spreading of this virus, this wonderful community's caregivers were not permitting family members of these residents to visit on site. In an attempt to stave off an outbreak within the community, the residents were also not permitted to go to their family's homes for the weekends as they had been used to doing prior to Covid-19. Not seeing loved ones was hard to deal with for these residents and we as family, but ultimately, it was a safe and wise thing to do.

Approximately three months went by before visits were allowed again and could only occur with proper precautions – PPE (personal protective equipment), social distancing, and limited time slots. I am happy to report none of the residents contracted the virus to my knowledge. They were cloistered, unable to attend day programs that enriched and nurtured them cognitively, physically, and artistically as previously scheduled before the pandemic. Like many other students in various educational environments, they too were taught through distance learning via electronic means and the creativity of their caregivers.

Before this pandemic, while on a home visit for the weekend in 2019, it struck me suddenly, how the light from the lamp by my daughter's bed, hit her face while tucking her in for the night. It fell on her joyful, smiling little face in such a way as though a halo had surrounded her. She looked so angelic. In an instant, I gasped inwardly, realizing the fortune and privilege I have had to be this young woman's mother all these years. I recalled so many memorable moments from her childhood – her accomplishments, her trials, her triumphs. I had been given such a gift to have witnessed them all. She truly is the HERO in this story! She and I giggled together as I blew air kisses on her neck, which tickled her and made the unfettered laugh she possesses come to life. Her infectious laugh always causes me to laugh. Much like yawning, it's contagious!

That evening tugged on my heartstrings, pulling out of me, a full range of emotions – a song of bittersweetness. Happy that she and I have lived through so many amazing years of action-packed, heart-stopping drama together, and sad because I had forgotten how my daughter's laughter sounded when she was a child. It was a cathartic moment. I had missed out on just how precious this person was, who I had birthed. I felt like I had been a faulty parent somehow, not remembering the many nuances from her childhood or her siblings' childhood, for that matter. I was always too *busy* doing whatever it took to ensure her and her siblings' survival during a very tumultuous and dark time in our lives. I had forgotten to stop and smell the roses, as they say. I often long for a *do-over* but sadly, that is reserved for rearview mirror, "pity-party" reflections – or as fate would have it…2020 vision. The *shoulda-woulda-coulda* jumps from time to time inside my head, cruelly reminding me of my messy imperfections as a young mother of the past.

By having the experience of being a mother of three children, one of whom was born unexpectedly born with Down syndrome, it is my hope that this book will positively impact or inspire first-time parents of their child with special needs to try and do life just a little bit better than I did. I feel it is important to point out through my own experiences, the do's and don'ts of navigating the unexpected diagnosis of such a challenging birth. Of course, if you have more than one child, your other children's needs should not be put on the back burner while attending to your child with special needs on a daily basis. There will be times when this becomes a challenging, delicate balancing act. The potential for resentment from your "normal" children towards you or their special needs sibling, may rear its ugly head when you least expect it from time to time in the future. Unfortunately, I know this all too well.

During the 1980s, I did not have the good fortune of owning the modern-day conveniences of a computer, the internet, Google search, or smartphones. If I am not mistaken, those things were just beginning to become viable to the average American household. I know, because my first husband had his first computer (a TRS 80 from Radio Shack by late 1970's). I believe I would have been better off organizationally as well as educationally, if these technological miracles had been at my disposal. I would have nurtured my little ones, including Kristina, to be much further ahead in a myriad of positive ways.

Looking back, I can honestly admit through these public and vulnerable thoughts, I almost sank the boat many times, while trying to sail without a prayer, a plan, support, or guide book. *Winging it*, was not always the best strategy for my situation. I wished I'd have done better. My desire is to help you avoid the pitfalls, missteps, and messy mistakes that I made.

Once, when Kristina was just an infant, I experienced a peculiar scene while in the waiting room of a specialist's office – a scene I will never forget. A young girl with Down syndrome, who was probably in her teens, was there with another woman I assumed was her mother. They had been sitting rather far apart from one another (as if COVID was already in existence back then). This is what I found to be peculiar. I couldn't imagine why this mother would want to be so distanced from her child in such a public place. To me, their interaction seemed cold. Viewing them both from a distance, I was filled with fear. Questions of doubt raced through my head. *How am I going to care for this child? What is going to happen to her? Is what I'm seeing going to be our future when she gets older?*

However, no sooner than those thoughts entered my mind, they were pushed aside by a quieter, more powerful voice that said, *"You're going to deal with this child one day at a time!"* At first, I was startled. This "voice" sounded so clear. It was as if someone behind me was whispering this message directly into my ear.

Back to that evening in 2019, when I was having a playful evening with my daughter, it occurred to me like a bolt of lightning had struck me! Those words *"one day at a time"* had arrived, staring back at me, right here, right then – surrounded by halos and laughter.

Life's journey had taken us through a bleak, dark time. I had pleaded with God many, many times for deliverance, strength, patience, more faith to successfully come out of this hell we had been experiencing, that quite possibly, I had created by my lack of good judgment. He answered my pitiful prayers in a big and beautiful way. Life for both of us looks more purpose-filled than nightmarish. I can now see clearly, God's plan for us, I feel blessed by the birth of (all my children) Kristina.

Throughout my adult life, because of her, she has kept me grounded, present and a reason to keep on living! Life is not lived in a straight or flat line. Hills, valleys and curves are meant to give meaning and depth to our personal growth. This is how I currently embrace all that we have experienced as a family throughout these past forty years.

I am looking UP now more than ever, and praising God for His ultimate wisdom over my life and the lives of my children every day. I feel thankful and have no regrets for having survived – and sometimes thrived – through these hardships and uncertainty. I am more grateful than ever for all that I have with Kristina and her siblings now.

Whoever reads my story, will hopefully be encouraged and enlightened. God will not give you more than you can handle. Yes, this is an old cliché, but it is true. You are not alone and don't have to go through this by yourself. There are many resources available and professionals in your area who are ready and willing to help keep you focused, organized, and on track while caring for your child with Down syndrome (or any other type of special needs) so that you may know, you've done all you can for your child's future

I pray, may YOU find knowledge, comfort and peace reading these words, and may your life be forever changed for the best. May you always look Up, be thankful, and be strengthened by our "Creators" infinite wisdom and care over all of our lives.

~~~Chapter One~~~

Generally speaking, many young adults (today or during my time in high school) may be tempted to think they *know it all*. Having barely graduated from high school, they believe they may be smarter than their parents. If young people are legally allowed at eighteen years of age, to join the military, vote, pay taxes, marry, then it is only natural for them to think they have a renewed advantage intellectually and otherwise over their predecessors! Many learn the hard way, that in fact, they do not. Why? They lack adult experiences.

Perhaps it could be argued, they may also suffer from a deficit in emotional intelligence as well as wisdom to know the differences between positive and negative decisions that may result in lifelong consequences. With a bit of luck and nurturing, young adults go forth in their daily lives, positively or negatively making impactful choices or decisions. With certainty, I can safely say, at one time, I was that young adult.

My high school boyfriend, and I were fresh out of high school, not yet eighteen. We decided it was a good thing to *legalize* being a couple after graduating. Our many unresolved, childhood issues were in stark contrast to one another with regard to our upbringing. How many times have we all heard that "opposites attract"? Individually, we had emotional deficits seemingly, unwittingly as wide as the Grand Canyon. Doubling that by being a couple, it would seem from an outsiders' perspective, bridging that wide and deep of a gap to form a solid connection would be impossible. We did the unthinkable, the impossible by getting married almost directly out of high school!

We met at the last high school I attended. It was the beginning of the second semester of our senior year at Northview High. I was singing, trying out for a musical, and he was the stagehand, doing the lighting. After tryouts, he rushed over to me – appearing as if out of thin air – and complimented me on my song choice and vocals. When he said I "blew him away" with my singing, I was dubious. I thought he was only trying to be kind or charm me. Taller than me, thin, sort of cute and wavy unkempt auburn hair, he wasn't dressed like a typical teenager of our time period. He wore polyester clothes and different color socks! (I found out later, he did his own laundry...it wasn't a *thing* like he tried to convince me it was!) Who does that? Most teens our age wore jeans and baggy tee shirts. There was evidence of a current acne breakout on his face and scars from past

~~~Chapter One~~~

Generally speaking, many young adults (today or during my time in high school) may be tempted to think they *know it all*. Having barely graduated from high school, they believe they may be smarter than their parents. If young people are legally allowed at eighteen years of age, to join the military, vote, pay taxes, marry, then it is only natural for them to think they have a renewed advantage intellectually and otherwise over their predecessors! Many learn the hard way, that in fact, they do not. Why? They lack adult experiences.

Perhaps it could be argued, they may also suffer from a deficit in emotional intelligence as well as wisdom to know the differences between positive and negative decisions that may result in lifelong consequences. With a bit of luck and nurturing, young adults go forth in their daily lives, positively or negatively making impactful choices or decisions. With certainty, I can safely say, at one time, I was that young adult.

My high school boyfriend, and I were fresh out of high school, not yet eighteen. We decided it was a good thing to *legalize* being a couple after graduating. Our many unresolved, childhood issues were in stark contrast to one another with regard to our upbringing. How many times have we all heard that "opposites attract"? Individually, we had emotional deficits seemingly, unwittingly as wide as the Grand Canyon. Doubling that by being a couple, it would seem from an outsiders' perspective, bridging that wide and deep of a gap to form a solid connection would be impossible. We did the unthinkable, the impossible by getting married almost directly out of high school!

We met at the last high school I attended. It was the beginning of the second semester of our senior year at Northview High. I was singing, trying out for a musical, and he was the stagehand, doing the lighting. After tryouts, he rushed over to me – appearing as if out of thin air – and complimented me on my song choice and vocals. When he said I "blew him away" with my singing, I was dubious. I thought he was only trying to be kind or charm me. Taller than me, thin, sort of cute and wavy unkempt auburn hair, he wasn't dressed like a typical teenager of our time period. He wore polyester clothes and different color socks! (I found out later, he did his own laundry…it wasn't a *thing* like he tried to convince me it was!) Who does that? Most teens our age wore jeans and baggy tee shirts. There was evidence of a current acne breakout on his face and scars from past breakouts, but that didn't bother me. Who was I to be so shallow, when I felt ugly, fat, and possessed two chipped front teeth due to a roughhousing incident during my childhood?

We introduced ourselves, and then he did the unspeakable – he asked me out! At the time, I didn't think anyone would ever want to date me, no thanks to my diminished view of myself. By this time, I had attended three different high schools because of being placed in three foster homes starting at the age of sixteen. Of course, I said yes, but not without my reservations. Arguing with my intuitions, which I ignored, I was about to discover what was lurking from his side of the fence.

My husband came from a typical upper-middle-class family of the 1970s. When we started dating, he showed me some of his baby pictures. He looked adorable as a child. He looked like the character Opie from *The Andy Griffith Show*, played by Ron Howard. It was easy to see why he was favored and spoiled for how cute and smart he was, by his parents. He was born in Covina, California, lived in one house with one set of parents. His family life on the surface bore a resemblance to the families we grew up watching on television, such as *Leave It to Beaver* or *Father Knows Best*. When he introduced me to his family, they seemed like the perfect picture of a stable family, while my family was the opposite. I enjoyed meeting them, though scared, and was taken aback by how warm and friendly they seemed…at first. Their house was stylish and roomy, a blaring contrast to what I had been accustomed to while living with my mother *and* after being placed in foster homes, which weren't exactly model homes either. I thought I had hit the proverbial jackpot of boyfriends by dating him, because his side of the fence seemed rich compared to my side. He was allowed to drive and would pull up to my driveway at my current foster home in a Lincoln Town Car. It felt like I was being picked up in a limousine! All I had ever known were busted up Volkswagens or station wagons with blown head gaskets!

After several weeks into our courtship, I started to noticed a shift in his family's attitude toward me. The more they got to "know" me, the more the warmth I first felt started to dissipate, especially from his mother. I know this was taking a toll on my then-boyfriend as he continued to make excuses for why he didn't invite me over regularly. Once, he said something that I knew was straight out of her mouth, and it continued to feed my insecurities.

His mother considered me to be from the "wrong side of the tracks" after learning about my foster home experiences. She insinuated this through her plethora of passive-aggressive comments that she made when my boyfriend wasn't around. She mostly frowned at the fact that I came from a broken (divorced) family. Back in the 1970s, most things societally, were buttoned up pretty tight. Looking back, it was during the Vietnam War and Nixon fiasco. In retrospect, I think people were trying to keep what seemed to be "happy days" in the 1950s and 60s tightly packed and closed to themselves, never leaking out real frustrations or fears. No one dared discuss lost moral compasses back then. If someone dared share anything intimate, they would be shunned by others for perceived immorality. My then-boyfriend's family fit that category quite well – moral, Italian, faithful Catholics, and biased in every way, in favor of their way of living life.

These evident disparities started to emerge the more we dated. For instance, while my mother was physically and emotionally abusive, his mother was passive-aggressive and sickly sweet to your face. His father worked in a thriving insurance industry. My mother worked in a donut shop, or a glass factory, or a restaurant, or whatever she could hold down for more than six months at a time. While his father read *The Los Angeles Times* as he sipped classy bourbon served over ice by his wife, my mother drank anything alcoholic and usually straight from the container in which it was purchased. While my husband's father was served dinner in the dining area, flanked by his doting wife and three children, my mother usually served us the riot act – either throwing our dinner on the table while utilizing every filthy word imaginable or dumping the food in the trash. Many times, one of us usually went to bed without eating.

My mother would be out carousing around, bringing home her "newfound friends" like an alley cat, calling them "Uncle So and So". In contrast, my then-boyfriend's parents had been faithfully married at least twenty years by the time

I met him. Eventually, my mother's "mates" would break up with her and leave, but not before having their way with my sisters or me. (But that's another story for a different time and possible book.) As I mentioned earlier, my husband and I were complete opposites and it can safely be said that our opposites distracted, detracted, and ultimately became destructive.

    My then-boyfriend and I had been dating four months and nearing the end of our senior year in high school. While on dates, he often confided in me about his apparent struggles and difficulties with his parents…not unusual given that many teenagers suffer from what they perceive as parental powers over them! Because he had no obvious plans to attend a university after graduation, or had any ambitions toward gainfully being employed, his father's threats of kicking him out after graduation loomed large and in charge in his mind. Somehow, my boyfriend got an "a ha" moment and surprised his parents (and me) by joining the Navy without their permission or knowledge. Shortly after graduation, he was abruptly shipped out for basic training in San Diego. Meanwhile, I was shipped off to my last foster home – not because of anything on my part, but because my third foster parents were moving further south. I had been awarded a scholarship for being a "good" foster kid just before graduation. I had plans to attend a junior college in Los Angeles County where I resided with a new foster family. I enrolled and started attending by late August, wanting to major in music performance. I had big plans to become a music major and opera star.

He succeeded and completed boot camp (barely...as he didn't possess an athletic bone in his body!) in October of 1974. As per his request, his family begrudgingly invited me to travel with them to attend his graduation ceremony. He appeared out of a sea of dress blue recruits, handsomely dressed, in his Navy Blues and shiny shoes. That night, we all went out to dinner at some swanky restaurant. That is when he suddenly proposed to me, in front of his (disapproving) parents. They were awestruck, mouths gaping open and not in a good way – especially since we only dated for a short period of time. Once we were alone after that fiasco of a dinner, he asked me to marry him again. This time, his request was fashioned in the most peculiar way: *"Karen, marry me, because if you don't, you know you will end up being a loose woman, pregnant, out of college and options."* Because I lacked so much in the way of self-respect and esteem, I thought his offer was something I couldn't pass up. How could I so stupidly refuse? He was right, right? After all, that is what I experienced in my home environment during my formative years. That must be how I would end up. And in my mind, he loved me enough to propose. Therefore, why not accept his offer to marry him?

My presence in my then-boyfriend's life was not wanted or welcomed by his parents. His abrupt marriage proposal caused a deeper seed of hatred within his mother's heart against me. In spite of his parents' disapproval, he had continued his persistence in wooing me. Like typical teenagers who thought they knew it all, I thought or believed he would be good person and partner for me. I thought...he was really in love...with me. In all actuality, it turns out, he being young, impulsive and emotionally inexperienced, was "in love" with the idea, not necessarily, the actionable commitment or follow through with me.

~~~Chapter Two~~~

Madly in love, we all scurried about to put together a church wedding soon after his boot camp graduation. He had orders to continue his naval career someplace else rather quickly. We married in November, 1974. I signed on the dotted line in the pastor's office, thereby signing my life away to my husband. I was forever his, or so I naively thought.

As newlyweds, we felt a new sense of independence, free from parental rebuke or report. However, we… in our naivety, traded our real parents for new ones by being newly classified as a military family. We were now considered "Property of the United States Government". We were sent by orders of the military on their direction, not ours, to fulfill *their* requirements. (I often thought, *I* joined the Navy without doing the boot camp thing. Indirectly, I guess I did.) As a newly married couple, our wants, desires, and needs were secondary. Our commitment to each other came last.

Often, I wondered why the military hadn't instructed their recruits to *not* get married right out of boot camp. But rather, to wait before making such a lifetime commitment at such a young age. Many like my husband, thought it was a sound idea to marry, because one got paid more and could live off the base, having just a little more independence and money than their peers. I guess that request or command would be a bridge too far for the military to require such instruction for their young recruits.

We did not have a clue what was about to unfold. No one comes into this world equipped with a manual on how to be an adult or married, for that matter. Wouldn't it be nice, if life was as organized as visiting your local department of motor vehicles, picking up a manual, studying the content, and passing a driver's test, thus receiving your driver's license? That would be a phenomenal way of living, if life truly worked out that way…like heaven! For me, the closest thing to an instructional manual on how to live life, was (and still is) the Bible…or for many others, whatever spiritual guide (or not) they feel comfortable utilizing. Otherwise, we all just have to punt or pivot with the tools given when we departed out the doors of our parents' house. Adding to that proverbial "toolbox" of life, is left up to the daily choices or decisions we make along the way.

At first, we didn't mind that the military sent us to various parts of the country. Neither of us had gone anywhere significant, or memorable, during our young lives. We were anxious to explore new places and meet new friends. I thought the Navy would be good for him and me because I'm a people person and love to travel. But, when my husband finished one training, we would have to pick up and move again. Moving got old and frayed our nerves. It seemed no sooner than we got settled, we would have to leave the friends we made, find new housing, and get lost in yet another unfamiliar town because we didn't have the convenience of a GPS or MapQuest back then. Instead, we used old-fashioned map books. We went to what seemed to be, so many different places in six years' time. From San Diego to Vallejo, California, to Idaho Falls, Idaho, then to Newport News, Virginia, and back to San Diego.

Due to the types of schools or trainings my husband had to attend, I would often find myself with plenty of time on my hands, alone and without emotional support. Our parents, though reachable by phone, were so far away and not readily available to rely on. My husband was usually gone for fifteen hours at a time in Idaho. I didn't mind that so much, as I had come accustomed to being alone and lonely in foster homes. I liked not having to be accountable to parents or foster parents. I enjoyed learning to be my own person and being a (Navy) wife. My husband and I would argue, but there weren't much to fight over – perhaps just over frivolous, immature things since he was gone most of the day.

I found myself pregnant while in Vallejo California. My first child was born in Idaho Falls, Idaho. We had been married just over a year and a half by this time. I gave birth to our son on June 2, 1976. My son's birth occurred three days prior to one of the worst manmade natural disasters to befall

Idaho. This was a cataclysmic event! The Teton Dam had failed and caused enormous devastation to property, livestock, and people. I was a first-time mom three months shy of my twentieth birthday.

Being a new mom, quickly released out of the hospital to nurture and nurse my baby, I was scared and felt a bone-chilling uncertainty upon witnessing so much death and destruction. With dead cattle and other destroyed debris making it look like an apocalyptic movie, I felt this mirrored my current state of mind. I didn't realize it then; I might have been suffering from postpartum depression.

I felt as though I hadn't received much in the way of compassion or empathy from my husband, or my doctor for that matter. My husband was very busy, no thanks to his long days of training and his renewed habit of smoking pot. I will say his choices became more skewed when he reintroduced himself to regularly smoking marijuana. He had always smoked this stuff as a rebellious teenager, under his parents disapproving nose (which explains to some extent, the reason for their constant power struggles between them and their son, in addition to our dating), but quit long enough to join the Navy.

The Navy didn't seem to be as strict about drug enforcement back in the 1970s as they are now. This habit reared its ugly head when our landlord, who owned the duplex we rented, gave my husband some of his stash. While our landlord was a full-time practicing pot-head, his wife was a faithful, practicing Mormon. The conflict between his faith, his desire to smoke pot as well as his marriage seemed obvious. I hadn't realized when we moved to Idaho that most faith-based churches there in Idaho were Mormon. I wasn't really attending any church at that time and never felt led to attend any of their services, though I was invited many times by our landlord's wife.

    I have the full advantage of looking back some forty-plus years, and I'm pretty sure our time in Idaho is where the train left the station for us as a couple. With my husband often smoking pot, this left me feeling like an outsider because I didn't participate or wasn't considered "cool" like our landlord or others who imbibed with my husband. I didn't like or approve of his regular consumption or how it left him acting strange, not present for us as a family. He was either too sleepy and stayed in bed for hours on the weekends, or stuck in some intellectually impaired loop or fog. It was as if his pot smoking kidnapped the original guy I married. Then again, I remembered, that there was that one red flag while we dated, I ignored. I was either too naïve to object, or, because I knew nothing about cannabis, never having used it myself. I thought it would be a passing fancy, and this habit would work itself out eventually and disappear. I was completely wrong. Later in life, I believe, this over consumption, contributed to his future, overall mental health.

    Shortly after the Teton Dam disaster, the Navy informed my husband that we were moving again. Before relocating, we went to visit his parents, introducing them to their new grandson. During our time there, his mother would make unkind, disingenuous remarks, such as, "*At least you waited until you were married to have a baby,*" and "*I halfway expected you and my son would be unwed parents. Are you sure it's his?*" It took everything in me to control my impulse to say something as equally unkind or perpetrate some act of violence upon her. Believe me when I readily admit, I thought of plenty to do and say in those instances, but instead, I would just walk away. Later, I would express my hurt feelings and frustration with my husband. Inevitably, we would end up arguing because virtually every time, he would defend his mother's actions, dismissing my feelings as if they weren't relevant or important. I interpreted his denial and defense of his mother as proof throughout our marriage. I was ecstatic when we finally departed his parents' house and set out for our new adventure. My husband would be stationed on the nuclear aircraft carrier in Virginia called the *Dwight D. Eisenhower*, during what's now currently referred to as the Vietnam Era.

    From this move, my vantage point, my sense of well-being had vastly changed. I felt as though I had come home. I had a déjà vu kind of feeling once we settled in. I felt safe, reenergized, filled with hope by the new possibilities of this place called Newport News. I, being originally from the state of Connecticut, loved the change of seasons! Fall being my most favorite of all because the trees turn from green to vivid reds, golden yellows, and bright orange as their leaves eventually dropped to the ground. This state so reminded me of my childhood.

We lived in a modest, two-bedroom apartment only a few miles from my husband's new assignment location. The ship my husband was ordered to serve on, was located at a very historic shipyard called Newport News Shipbuilding. I could see this magnificent ship being built on the dry dock from a hill above it. To me, it was incredible! Half of the ship had a thick metal skin over her frame, while the remaining half was exposed metal, much like a skeleton. (The female gender is traditionally assigned to ships or boats; Old superstition, from sailors long ago, I've learned.)

I loved looking down from this hill in Victory Landing Park. The entire area was steeped in rich history from our country's beginning. I couldn't wait to discover all there was to see and learn here. Many times, just for entertainment sake, I drove my son and I to visit this park just to bask in the progress and miracle of this sailing vessel. I had a childlike awe at witnessing this. What I could not see with my own eyes, my husband would give me detailed accountings of its progress when his day was through. I was mesmerized by his nightly, oral reports. Once the construction of this craft was finally completed, all of its sailors and many other military crews aboard, would sail to unknown shores all over the world. We civilians left ashore, were not allowed to know the exact location the ship was to travel, as that was classified information.

To occupy my time, I would take my son to the park across from the complex. This park had a big pond, full of migratory birds, healthily wooded with rich green forest foliage. My young son and I loved that park. We would find ourselves there often. To be there was like magic and a source of entertainment. My son would get chased by an aggressive goose on occasion, which he still recalls to this day. (forty-four years later!) We would also drive to nearby historic towns like Williamsburg and Virginia Beach. I loved traveling the lower level of the Chesapeake Bridge. Not only was that bridge scenic, it was iconic to the area. Ships simultaneously passed over us as we drove under and through the underwater tunnel. Virginia was my favorite place of all. I developed friends from attending church and befriended some Navy wives, who I met during my husband's occupancy on the ship.

I found myself pregnant...again! My second child, a girl, was born in March of 1979. Her father was out to sea during most of my pregnancy, which I was unusually grateful about. I spent many moments alone like most navy wives, having the sole responsibility of my children's safety and well-being on my shoulders. I had become accustomed to being the father, mother, and head of my household. My children and I would spend many hours outdoors at the park, the beach, or church. I found solace by being connected to other adults who were not necessarily associated with the military, especially since our families were on the other side of the continent.

      While my husband was on the ship, we stayed connected via snail mail (U.S. Postal Service) ... We didn't have the modern convenience of cell phones and the internet like we do today.) Six months before he was to take his last sea excursion, ending his naval career, he decided without my input, to moved us to San Diego, where he found an affordable apartment with the assistance from connections he had there. He had to do it this way, because if we had waited to move after he got out, the Navy wouldn't have covered the moving expenses.

      On his last tour of duty, I informed my husband I was pregnant, making this our third! I also called his parents out of obligation and consideration, to which his mother stated insultingly, if this child I am carrying, was her son's...again! This time, she went so far as to suggest I seek abortion services. She knew her son was about to depart from the Navy without future prospects of job security or financial stability. This insinuation or request, again, threw me into more self-doubt and rejection. After hanging up from talking with her, I felt a certain anxiety about our return. What made those hurtful suggestions that I seek an abortion even worse, coming from her; she was supposedly a devout catholic!

      Arriving in California, specifically San Diego, was quite the change from what I had been connected to for the last three years in Virginia. We had been in Newport News from the fall of 1976 until spring of 1980. The community in San Diego wasn't as green as I had become accustomed to in Virginia. There was way more traffic as well. I had to leave my friends, my church, my children's playground, and be uprooted once again. This move resulted in us being closer to my husband's parents, who lived in Orange County, an hour and a half away. Not far enough in my mind. There was a silver lining though. I found out my third foster parents lived close in the next community over from his parents. I'd had a close relationship with them throughout the years despite the fact I had to leave their foster home and go to another – my fourth and last. They were in a sense, my substitute parents and my children's "grandparent" too!

My husband while in Virginia, found our two-bedroom apartment, in a section of San Diego called Normal Heights. Who does this? Naming a place NORMAL! It was sort of quaint, but everywhere I went in San Diego there seemed to be people on top of people, good areas (like La Jolla), and not so nice areas, like any other city I assume. Back then, San Diego was considered to be relatively small town compared to the sprawling city of Los Angeles just up the coast 3 hours away. Again, I would seek out the parks, playgrounds, and the beaches, which were our sources of entertainment since our financial situation from the Navy was about to end. I made friends with various neighbors in

Normal Heights, one of whom (unknowingly) would later prove to be toxic.

While waiting for my husband's return, I would tease my young children telling them, "Daddy will be home soon!" They would squeal in delight every time I said this. My son was four, and my daughter had just turned two. We had established ourselves in our little apartment and new community, making friends, going to church, and staying loosely connected with my husband's parents during his absence. Once he arrived home for good as a civilian, his plan was to set immediately to either find work or go to college. After having many conversations with his father, he finally settled on finding a job. His father made it abundantly clear that college would have to wait.

We took the kids to his parents and went on a mini vacation to his grandmother's cabin up further north. While there, my husband read books and didn't communicate much. I just took his emotional distancing as his way of decompressing and regrouping. I spent time alone, going for walks in the woods, with my abdomen swelling by the moment it seemed. We couldn't do much else because again , we were being careful with what little money we had saved before his departure from the military. Once we got back home, he would go into panic mode trying to find work because again, his father made it clear that he wasn't supporting us, not even with a loan!

~~~Chapter Three~~~

After my husband's father's rather icy hot proclamation that he wasn't going to support us financially, miraculously, it was around that time my husband found a job. He told me this on my birthday in September, not more than six weeks after his final departure from the Navy. Out of the blue, he asked me to go on a walk, down to a local park. I was suspiciously optimistic, but thought he was being rather nice because it was my birthday, given the fact he had been emotionally unavailable during our vacation. Or, perhaps he would enlighten me further and tell me more about what he thought our future was going to hold, since he found employment.

I called my friend (I had made during his absence) to babysit. She consented, and we were off on our walk. With my very pregnant belly, we didn't walk fast or far. We ended up on a bench attached to a small community library, where the sun had been warming the wall that I was about to lean up against. The breeze was gently blowing, and the warmth of the bench and wall made me feel cozy and supported. The sun politely hit my face while the warm breeze, whisked my long hair behind me.

During our walk, my husband had been talking to me about superficial things. He seemed animated, happy. I thought he was going to share some exciting news about his employment results. I fully expected he was going to surprise me in a good way on my birthday, not suspecting for one second what was about to unfold. He surprised me alright! Once we arrived at the library, sat down, his mood shifted and he suddenly got serious. He started the conversation by stating rather robotically, how much he loved me and the kids, further explaining how concerned he was about our financial future. I was looking for him to tell me about a promising future, but instead, he went on to say that he was in love with someone else!

As my face became crestfallen, the color draining from my expression, he hurriedly explained, he wanted to be upfront and honest. When I asked with whom, he further gut-punched me by stating it was our neighbor, who was currently watching our children. I couldn't help but feel sick to my stomach, gripped with sudden fear. I started sobbing inconsolably, with long strands of moisture coming from my nose like a flash flood. I am presuming, he thought I would be happy by this confession, since we spent most of our marriage arguing about stupid, petty things. I asked if she knew. He denied she was aware of his feelings. He said it was his intention to be honest and open with her, with me about his feelings, and would let her know as soon as we got home. He said, he had no idea how she was going to react after his declaration of love for her. He was hoping for the best results…of course!

The walk home seemed like hours, miles, an eternity. The feeling of intense dread came upon me. Barely able to walk, I was bent over every so often, in sobbing waves. The way I felt, he might as well had kicked me right where I was growing our baby. I struggled to get home. He was also struggling to get me home too, but for a different reason. All I wanted to do, was crawl into bed, pull the blankets over my head, and hope to disappear or be transported to another planet.

Suddenly, I was in the throes of a chaos that I had not seen coming. Broadsided and in sheer panic, I don't think I slept for two weeks straight. I lost eight pounds from the stress, not being able to eat. At one point, I thought I would lose the baby growing in my abdomen from "spotting" due to being so unhinged. My children lost their father living at home with us, and I lost my husband to my supposed friend. She had the option of saying no under the circumstances. Instead, selfishly she said yes, altering all our lives permanently.

Having forced to being neighbors with her and my husband, suddenly seemed claustrophobic. I felt trapped. It wasn't like I could move, especially being six months pregnant. When he left, he kept his finances too. Depriving me of his financial support, put my little family in jeopardy of being homeless and starving. I had to go on public assistance in order to prevent that from happening. He had no trouble finding money for his new love interest – paying for a new engagement ring, courting her with romantic rides in a limousine, and treating her kids with gifts while mine went without. I threatened to convey his whereabouts to the welfare department, he would retaliate with more financial damage. He took the car from me, further strangling me financially and isolating me socially. I was restricted as to my daily movement out and about, unless he "let" me go or drove me where ever I needed! I felt imprisoned by my own husband. Thankfully, my foster family stepped in to help and assisted me with their used car later.

Eventually, though, his whereabouts were revealed by my confession to the welfare department. He was forced to face his responsibilities, even if that meant the government had to deduct child support from his wages. He of course, was angry, embarrassed as a result of this action I took. He had to pay back the three months of arrears to the welfare department and continue to pay future payments. This consequence meant he and his new girlfriend wouldn't be able to relocate as soon as they would have liked…away from me and the kids.

For the several months, my children, her children, and our neighbor's children were privy to the many arguments that ensued. My young children, once happy to have their father home, were now unhappy and confused with why their daddy was living next door; all of us coexisting in chaos. Jerry Springer would have been more than happy to have us as guest on his show if he had known our situation. Our fights, arguments, and drama would have surely won Jerry a daytime Emmy!

The months dragged on in one sense and sped by in another. Finally, December crawled up. I was supposed to have my baby in the middle of the month, leaving me time to try and provide some semblance of a nice Christmas for my children. My due date whizzed by, and before I knew it, Christmas was upon us. So was our baby! I woke in pain (not unusual given the current situation). The day had finally arrived, amidst this storm of noise and undue stress. December 23, 1980, *would have* been somewhat of a joyful event to celebrate had it not been for the fact my child was born on my husband's girlfriend's birthday! Ten days past my due date and right on time for more chaos, Kristina was born. The Christmas story in the Bible seemed farfetched in their seemingly adverse situation, giving birth to Jesus. I felt as if the birth of my daughter, though not comparable in many respects, was somehow similar on the human suffering side of things. To me, my situation was no Christmas miracle, but that of a Christmas nightmare

~~~Chapter Four~~~

Traveling to the hospital with my estranged husband, was uncomfortable on so many levels. I tried not convey the pain I was experiencing. I tried not to utter a word or sound while he drove! To be in labor in front of a guy who left you for the next-door neighbor, in my mind, was as absurd as giving birth in front of a bank robber in the active process of robbing the bank! His girlfriend stole my husband, and my husband stole our marital status as well as our future, by accepting this bizarre situation. At this point, though we had just spent six years together, he might as well have been a complete stranger. This difficult person I married and currently separated from; did not deserve the intimacy a normal, happily married couple would be experiencing at that moment. I didn't want him to see me vulnerably in pain. Therefore, on the way to the hospital, I secretly decided I would deny him of that privilege. I requested the doctor give me an epidural, wiping out any possibility of a pain filled event for me to have to endure, while he stood there stupidly observing.

As quickly as labor had started, it was over. My child was born. My other children, born without complications, looked similar to one another. I expected the same for this newborn. I had carried her full term; my expectations were that everything would be as it was the other two times…normal.

When my daughter arrived, the doctor asked us what we wanted to name our child. While in route to the hospital, I also made another crucial decision. I would not allow my husband to choose this child's name, as he had done with our other two children. Before my husband could utter a word, I quickly stated, "Kristina." My husband added Alexandria as her middle name, and because I liked it, I allowed it.

I barely got a quick glance at our slow-to-cry baby. I noticed she had a lot of dark hair and seemed to have a more bluish red complexion. Before my daughter was taken away, I also noticed how flat her nose was, and her eyes; they were slanted. Her hands were wide and her fingers, stubby. I also could see that her little toes on her feet were not uniformly shaped. The last three toes were shorter than usual.

The nurse whisked her away, before I could ask questions, to check her vitals, weight, and clean her up…or so I thought. The doctor worked on me, while the pediatrician worked with the nurses on my daughter. They conveyed her weight was average: seven pounds, four ounces. They didn't say anything more, other than they were checking a few things and it would be a while. Since I was being distracted by my doctor helping me, I didn't think anything necessarily alarming, except to say I noticed how different Kristina looked, compared to my other two children. I just thought the way they were tending to my child, was standard procedure for all newborns.

Shortly thereafter, I was wheeled into a hospital room I expected to share with another mother. However, I was alone. A few hours went by, and suddenly, my husband strode into my room with flowers for me, placing them on a table at the foot of the bed. I thanked him and asked about our baby. Had he seen her yet? He said he had and that he had met with the pediatrician. After a quick pause, he blurted out, "Kristina is a mongoloid!" He might as well have said our baby was an alien from some other planet in a galaxy far, far away! With that, he stood up, pivoted around military style, and walked out, not waiting for any questions or emotional reaction from me. I could imagine, he had some explaining to do with his girlfriend who was waiting impatiently for his arrival with our other children at her house…next door!

Alone…I was left to wonder was this our fault, specifically mine because of all the stress I was going through? On our many trips to the store, while pregnant and separated, we would passionately argue in the car. I vividly remember, it was raining and there was a young adult standing at the front of the store outside waiting for whomever. I vaguely remembered; this person resembled the group of people I saw at the park in Virginia with similar features. I pointed this person out to him, shouting "I hope...we don't have one of *those*!" I vaguely thought I knew what the term "mongoloid" meant. Similar features and cognitively childlike, but I wasn't sure if he meant that was *our* baby. After he abruptly left, I was overcome with guilt, uncertainty and dread. Left alone to worry, my imagination ran wild.

All at once, a wave of white coats descended upon my tiny hospital room. While people were crammed from wall to wall, shoulder to shoulder in this small space of a hospital room, I felt enveloped and claustrophobic. One by one, everyone introduced themselves, listing their gifts and talents after their names. The gravity and seriousness of this scene suddenly hit me. I had never experienced such attention when I gave birth to my other children. This medical army of professionals, introduced themselves one by one, which felt like it took forever, while I tried to listen intently. I was actually scared at this point, waiting for the other shoe to drop...and it did...like a bomb!

The pediatrician who had attended to my baby informed me that my daughter was born with Down syndrome otherwise known as "mongolism". He also said he was worried about how my husband was taking the news. "Your husband seems to be taking this news rather matter-of-fact. Is he okay?" "How can a guy who leaves you for the next-door neighbor be okay with anything, much less this?" I replied sarcastically.

Without missing a beat, the doctor went on to say, "We feel it medically necessary to transfer your baby to the hospital next door where they can better serve her most pressing medical issues. We suspect she has a hole in her heart, which is common for babies born prematurely. Since she is not premature, we are concerned about her heart and oxygen levels. They don't seem quite right. However, we don't want to do anything until you inform us of how much you or how far, you want us to medically intervene for your baby?" I listened in shock and retorted as such! "I want you to do everything medically feasible to save my child! Whether she has Down syndrome or not, she's still my baby!" Were the doctors asking me permission to keep my baby alive with the way they structured their comment "how much do you want us to medically intervene?"

Each medical professional proceeded to explain why they were there and how it related to my baby. A heart specialist, the hospital social worker, medical students, and the pediatrician. The medical terms they used was more than any young mother could digest. What they were saying medically, might as well of been said in a French or Latin! I couldn't understand any of it! One by one, finishing each of their diagnosis and medical plans for my baby, vanished from my room as abruptly as they had arrived, leaving me to fall silently apart — sobbing into my pillow. A nurse intermittently came to check on me throughout her shift that night, asking me if I was alright and could she do anything for me. "Sure!"

I said, in a tearful response. "If you could arrange for me to be someone else, that would really help!" I could only imagine now, that this wasn't what occurred on her usual shift assignment and I can still remember, she was legitimately worried for and about me

The night of December 23rd seemed to last an eternity. While waiting to be released from my current hospital (not so hospitable stay) in order to see my newborn in the next hospital over, I was busy making a few important phone calls Christmas Eve, to various family members…his side and mine. While conveying the news, the response I heard on the other end, went something like "we're so sorry" while crying or speechlessness… utter radio silence. No one offered to come by…no one offered to visit. No one knew what to do. I can't say that I blame them, as they had been listening to the separation saga before this birth. Now, this news of Kristina, only make the picture in their already frozen mind…worse. Before leaving the hospital that day, the case manager from the hospital, came by and handed me a long list of professionals to contact when my baby got home. She shook my hand, bid me good luck and left!

I had to wait to leave the hospital, like a horse waits to leave the starting gates at a derby. There were many false starts, literally zapping my energy from the fight-or-flight response. I was told numerous times I would be leaving any minute. Any minute, seemed like hours. It got to the point where I almost left on my own volition but I didn't have transportation. I was so desperate to go to the hospital next door that I was ready to pay someone to break me out. Finally, coordinating my exit with my husband's entrance so he could pick me up, was finally accomplished. We drove in silence to the nearby hospital five minutes away where my daughter was being cared for. Neither of us asked how the other was doing. I don't know about him, but I was deathly afraid of what was about to happen, once we set foot at our daughter's bedside.

Not long after we arrived to see our baby, right on cue, my husband's girlfriend arrived. As if pulled like a magnet toward her direction, he went to speak to her. I could see her talking with my husband down the hall while I waited impatiently for him to rejoin me. I was so angry and out of sorts that she would dare show up and be present at such a critical time. I'm sure she felt she was at a dangerous crossroads at this point in their new relationship. This drama wasn't in her plans either. She could lose her new love through this tragedy if her boyfriend, my husband, suddenly arrived at some renewed sense of his/our predicament and broke up with her, to come back with us. I had to pretend that she wasn't there while a neonatal nurse greeted us. She escorted us to our baby's bedside. I was never so secretly happy that SHE (the girlfriend) couldn't come in. It was all I could do not to look over in her direction to give her some murderous death stares. Remembering where I was, I stopped focusing on her watching our every move through the glass wall, as we followed the nurse who took us to our daughter.

A television series I enjoyed watching, started in 1972 called M*A*S*H. The reason for this "memory lane recall" is that in some weird way, our baby's hospital surroundings reminded me of that show. The scene I experienced while entering this space was amazing technologically speaking, drama filled and emotionally overwhelming. Nothing short of a weird mix of "twilight zone" science fiction and medical drama experience. The NICU, an ICU for babies at this hospital, was in a huge room filled with fragile babies lying in special, technologically adapted beds. Many warning buzzers and bells were going off, crying babies, tubes and machines attached to these crying souls and the hum of low talking filled the air as nurses, doctors, and parents gathered around the various beds of these tiny, helpless newborns.

As if in slow motion, we finally arrived at the location where our baby's doctor was holding our child, trying to intubate her. My little girl was fighting against his efforts by gagging, but he kept on working. I was caught off guard at how unconcerned he was at our presence. I don't think he knew we were there watching him work on our daughter. To my vantage point, he was quietly focused on his patient, determined to successfully get the intubation done quickly.

Out of the blue, I felt faint from the enormity of it all. I started to fall against my husband. He fought to keep me upright, chastising me for making a scene and warning that I was embarrassing him. I'm sure he was referring to being embarrassed in front of his chaperone/girlfriend who was watching us intently from across the room…of course. Desperately needing to sit down, my husband led me to a seat at the side of the room, where I woozily watched the doctor complete his task. (Now looking back, I wished I had the strength to stand up to my husband and let him know his presence was not welcomed, especially with his girlfriend tagging along beside him. I tried my best to remain stoic, resolving to keep it together.)

Seeing I was overcome, the doctor came over to me once the baby was secure, and explained what he was doing for our newborn. Though I barely understood what he said, I didn't have the presence of mind to take notes. But then, who thinks to pull out a notebook to take notes in that situation anyway? He told us Kristina had a heart condition common in premature babies, which I now know as Patent Ductus Arteriosus, a hole in the heart, that with time, would eventually close. If not, it could be surgically corrected in most cases depending on the severity. He further explained that the hospital staff would be keeping a close eye on her blood gases, as not enough oxygen was pumping through her body, which was causing her blueish color. He continued to educate us about the future for Kristina, possibly having many other medical surprises appear as she aged. He listed some of them as possibilities, but as time would have it, I would come to find out that many of what he listed were altogether different.

Kristina would be in her techno bed for two long weeks, battling to survive, and I was there alongside her every day. After a week, her intubation was unnecessary as her heart condition improved. I was allowed short periods of time to hold her while attempting to bottle feed her. She had a difficult time sucking or swallowing, par for her intubated condition. I spoke to her, trying to reassure her that I was there for her, sung little lullabies to her, and touched her as much as I could. She was so tiny and fragile, tubes coming from her little body everywhere it seemed. While holding her, I took in every detail of her appearance that I could, as well as her utterances. I used to cry upon seeing her every day I returned. I hated leaving her side, frightfully wondering if one of those days, would that be our last time together.

If it hadn't been for the nurses so thoughtfully decorating the place, I wouldn't have even remembered it was Christmas or New Year's. Sometimes when I left the hospital late at night, the atmosphere outside looked gloomy, giving it a foggy London kind of feel. Many a night, after giving myself the difficult permission to leave my baby's bedside, I ordered a breakfast sandwich from Jack in The Box. Forty years later, that fast food place is still there in the same place. Driving by it, reminds me of how I'd wolf down that sandwich without a thought of a healthy diet during this chaotic time. Self-care was a luxury that I couldn't afford at the time. I drive by it these days, with the ghost of Christmas past, thankfully in the rearview mirror, ever grateful for what I have now.

Much later, past all this drama, while taking an English class at a junior college, I wrote a paper about children born with Down syndrome and learned a plethora of information. Before 1980, many medical doctors were left with the decision of whether or not to perform heart surgery on kids born with this syndrome. Their attitude toward children who had Down syndrome or other developmental disabilities was that they weren't going to be productive members of society later in life, so why bother…unless the parent insisted that they medically intervene. Thankfully, it's an unethical practice for a doctor to withhold medical treatment of any kind due to someone's disability.

~~~Chapter Five~~~

During the early stages of my daughter's infant life, I took the word of most doctors as the gospel truth. Who was I to argue with a trained professional? They spoke, and I implemented their advice as best I could. I felt medically illiterate and ill equipped to care for this child with all her many medical, or cognitive issues. There were no social media or Google as we know it today, where I could arm myself with some semblance of knowledge when anything occurred concerning her health and overall wellbeing.

There was truly little knowledge shared or available to support me. I wasn't focused beyond who or where I could turn in order to tackle most of my daughter's more pressing cognitive or health issues, except to go to doctors who supposedly knew. There was the church for support, the library to get more information, or case managers who worked for an organization called The San Diego Regional Center, specifically there to service families with children who had special needs. These people were specifically trained to do the work of many…basically overloaded with cases and worthy of running for the hills if one stayed too long at this career.

There were Down syndrome support groups where you could align yourself with parents who had children born with the same syndrome. However, after a while, the novelty of my attendance wore off because most of the parents started turning the group's focus to their marital burdens. With my own failing marriage, I felt helpless and overwhelmed as to how to help them by my attendance, or benefit by continuing to attend and listen to other people's marital problems. Sometimes I wondered if I had stepped into an AA meeting instead of a support group for parents who had children like mine. Looking back, parents at that time were just as much in a "deer-in-headlights" mode as I was and trying to keep it together. One couple I got to know ended up divorcing not long after their child was born.

At the time, I didn't know, just in the United States, there were approximately 6,000 babies born…one in 700 babies, with Down syndrome, *each year*! (I learned this after attending college classes while all my children were in school and I was on public assistance) This was shocking to learn. Equally as shocking to learn, was doctors' attitudes regarding fixing heart problems. Before the 1980s, medicine and the medical community seemed out of the "Dark Ages" with regard to treating children with special needs. Medical professionals seemed very conservative with children born with any type of cognitive or physical defects. Many medical professionals thought these children, if they survived the first year, would be better served behind institutional walls.

I had one such (older) doctor in not-so-subtle a manner, inform me, I should consider placing Kristina in an institution, while examining her. He said my other two children (who were with me in the exam room and "bouncing off the walls") would not get a fair shake in this life if I kept Kristina home with us. In other words, he believed all my attention would go to her and not to my other "normal" children. Of course, I was highly insulted and complained of his comment to his supervisors! He was right in one sense. Kristina garnered much attention, through no fault of her own. When there are two parents, parenting can hopefully be shared, but when there is only one, then care for all of one's children is unbalanced. The one who "yells" the loudest and the most typically gets the most attention.

In the first two years of my daughter's life, it seemed all we ever did, was go to various medical specialists. It kept me busy. Just for the record, Kristina was seen by a pediatrician, a pediatric cardiologist, an eye care specialist, a neurologist, a gastroenterologist, a speech and hearing specialist, and an E.N.T specialist during the first few years. Later, when she was seven years old, she saw a specialist for her bladder.

By the time Kristina was four months old, she was wearing tiny glasses for a condition known as strabismus (crossed eyes) and atrophy of her optic nerves, which means she would eventually go blind. She also was on medications for small seizures that started during a doctor's visit. Luckily for her (and me), she had a seizure while in the waiting room, in front of the doctor. These seizures occurred whenever and where ever, and were not the noticeable type such as a "grand mal seizure". The medication she was put on, changed her demeanor drastically, making her irritable and sleepy. This medication is still being used for other types of conditions today, but Kristina is no longer on them due to a condition I will speak on a little later in this chapter.

Since I took Kristina to so many appointments, the doctors knew us well. Most were helpful to me and my daughter, but if I found that one had a less than favorable attitude about kids with special needs, they would no longer be my daughter's doctor. Sometimes, her pediatrician would kid me about how fastidious I was about Kristina's care. He thought I was being a helicopter mom, meaning I was being overly concerned about her health.

On one such occasion, before she turned two, I spoke with her pediatrician about my concerns. I thought Kristina wasn't thriving. I felt her growth had slowed and that she wasn't interested in walking or sitting up. I was genuinely concerned, but the pediatrician countered my concern by saying Kristina wasn't going to hit various physical and cognitive benchmarks as do "normal" children. Of course, this distressed me and caused me to feel sad for my daughter. I insisted to him that I understood this and that I thought her non-thriving was possibly due to her seizures or the medication prescribed.

The pediatrician referred me back to her original cardiologist whose name was Dr. Kishanni, an excellent, renowned heart specialist. He was so kind and compassionate toward Kristina...probably to all his pediatric patients. Regardless, I shared with him my "motherly intuition" regarding my daughter, and he said, "Karen, if you honestly think there is something else going on with her heart, it is worth a look, in order to dispel any of your fears." Never was I so relieved, that someone actually cared that much, to take the extra step necessary to rule out any of my intuitive nudging's about Kristina's overall health and well-being.

Her surgery was scheduled for October of 1982, as long as she remained flu or cold free. Her cardiologist performed a scope from her groin to her heart which would look inside the heart. This could be risky because she had to have an epidural in order to stay absolutely still for the procedure. I offered to help hold her while the doctor's assistant inserted the needle in her back. I couldn't believe how strong Kristina had suddenly become. I struggled to hold her in a fetal like position. I honestly thought I was about to faint from the stress and length of time it took to hold this child still. She tried her best to put up quite the fight. We finally succeeded and not a moment too soon. I was sweating alongside the doctor, who told me to go and sit down as my face looked gray as a ghost.

After Dr. Kishanni performed the procedure, he came out with a confident smile and some good news. He said she had a condition that was rare for "normal" people, and never with Down syndrome. Apparently, she had an extra artery on the outside of her heart where bacteria filled blood filtered directly to her brain, rather than through her lungs. But, from performing this procedure successfully, he found this condition and tied it off permanently.

Having another "ah ha" moment, I asked him, could that have been the reason why her seizures started at four months old. I think he realized that I may have been on to something from the question I asked him, but was not certain. He advised me to keep giving her seizure meds until the neurologist could do more testing. After a few months, if the heart surgery actually contributed positively to stopping these seizures, it would be more obvious then. Fortunately, my suspicions or intuitions were later confirmed correct about her condition and its relation to her failure to thrive. She would be permanently free of seizures and the medicine to treat them!

Shortly after the surgery, Kristina's personality changed to a more pleasant and thriving one. She seemed more interactive and aware of her surroundings. She laughed more with her siblings, who did their best to be kind, compassionate, funny, and helpful with their baby sister who was "different" and fragile. She has a lifelong scar going from the back of her shoulder blades to the front just underneath her breast, white from age, but still visible. Her scar is her badge of honor. It is a constant reminder to me, of just how precarious and precious her survival and life was then and still is now. After this delicate surgery, that's when I saw my daughter turn the corner from many of her initial medical issues. It's not like they disappeared in totality, but she outgrew most of them, making her more medically stable.

For the first two years, she always caught a cold, which would turn into croup, an ear infection, or both. She had to be treated surgically with tubes in her blown-out eardrums at least a couple of times a year. She had a mucus plug in the lower lobe of her lung, which earned her an extended stay for a week in the hospital. Kristina had surgery on her eyes to straighten them...twice. Later, when she was seven, she had a blood blister in her bladder that showed up out of nowhere and had to be cauterized! All the while she would be sick, I had to guess what was wrong since she couldn't verbalize to me that she was experiencing pain. One time, while shopping with her, she suddenly threw up! It wasn't that I was oblivious, but unless she overtly showed me that she was sick, I didn't know until the last second...mostly in inconvenient places. It was an adventure taking her anywhere, because I never knew what was going to occur...with her or her young siblings. Chaos was our first, middle, and last names. Traveling circus...that was what I felt we were! Her father...missing in (his) action always.

~~~Chapter Six~~~

Kristina was nearly two years old and barely over her major heart surgery, when I met my future husband in a not-so-romantic place. It was an unlikely, ordinary facility...the Laundromat. The day we met, my kids had taken over the place with their vocal outbursts, running around the washers and dryers, laughing and carrying on. Kristina was quietly laying in her car seat that I placed upon the table while folding everyone's clothes.

Up to this point, I'd had it with men. I wasn't looking and didn't care if I ever had one in my life again. My estranged husband and I were still married but separated, living next door to each other. He was trying to get another place but was having trouble financially because the Department of Child Welfare finally caught up with him, forcing him to pay child support as well as arrears. It was a very frustrating time for us all. It seemed; I couldn't catch a break, even if I could afford to purchase one!

Future husband walked in to do his laundry and couldn't *help* but notice me. Instead of getting to the task of doing his laundry, he came over to me and introduced himself...again. *"The last time we spoke, was at the grocery store. I have been trying to find you ever since!"* he quietly expressed. It was true we had met a few times before, either doing laundry or at the grocery store. I was in back of him in line at the grocery store one day with my kids in tow, when I said that I noticed he did laundry at the same place I did. He stood out to me especially because he was very tall and always had running shorts or other types of shorts on, during winter. I couldn't help but notice his long, muscular, bare legs each time I saw him and asked if he was a runner. He replied with a prideful "Yes" and explained he was a long distant runner. I lamely claimed, I liked running too (at the time) but wasn't always as consistent for obvious reasons...my kids and the lack of babysitters. After me and my parade left the store, I thought nothing more of this man, or our conversation.

    I was taken aback from his shy confession. *Him...trying to find me?* That, I thought, was a crazy notion. Thinking inwardly to myself, *"Did you not notice that I have my hands full?"* Instead of expressing what I was really thinking, I replied with a surprised *"Oh!"* He then asked the names of my (rambunctious) children. I hesitantly introduced them after they raced by us, making their running rounds about the washing machines. I also introduced him to "quiet" Kristina.

    He went on to say, when we had last spoken many weeks prior, I made such an impression on him and he couldn't stop thinking about me. He had attempted rapidly finish his transaction at the store that day, raced out the door to find me so we could talk more, but I had already disappeared. He also surmised; I must live somewhere close in the neighborhood. He said he drove his car up and down streets to see if he could find me, but that didn't yield success either. He also said, every time he went to the Laundromat, or the store, he would purposefully look for me. *"Why?"* was my dumbfounded response.

He shyly said, he found me cute, funny and wanted to get to know me better. I was blown away. At various times throughout my then current, chaotic situation, I thought, *No one is going to ever desire me, a single mother with three boisterous kids.* After years of being beaten down emotionally, I thought so little of myself. Though I was young, I felt washed-up, unavailable, unattractive on so many levels! For this reason, and the fact I had three young children, one with special needs, I found his interest in me, incredulous yet intriguing.

He asked if I was single, and I said not exactly, that I was separated and my husband lived next door to me and my children, with his girlfriend. I thought for sure, this would surely dissipate any further interest in me, but it didn't seem to dissuade him. I suppose he felt compassion for me, because he asked if we could date. *"What?! "You want to date ME?" "Do you not see what is happening here?",* referring to my tribe running wildly about the place. Figuring he wasn't serious, I told him if he wanted to go out with me, he would have to memorize my last name and look me up in the phone book. I was certain he wouldn't remember. Yet, to my utter surprise, he called two days later. It was right after Kristina's 2nd birthday on Christmas Eve, that he came into our lives so unexpectedly.

He was so thoughtful and sweet, bringing Christmas presents for all my children. We didn't even have a celebratory Christmas tree to put his gifts under, which prompted him to go out and purchase one. Later, shortly after Christmas, he asked us out on a date, which I relented and said yes. My children were excited of course, except me. I was scared and intrigued as to WHY this man would be the least bit interested in all of us, much less me.

He asked me out on several more dates, and rather quickly, more than I was comfortable with, became serious about me, *and* my traveling circus of a crew. He really bonded with Kristina and shared with me he too, had a half-sister who had Down syndrome. His father had been married before, placing a child he had had with his first wife, in an institution in New York. He told me, he never had the opportunity to visit his half-sister. If he did, he said he was too young to remember.

Soon after we started dating, he invited me to his father's house. His father took a quick liking to Kristina. He would make tickling noises while poking Kristina in her side, causing her to belly laugh. It made everyone happy to hear her laugh. I was overjoyed by the attention from him and his family, especially since what I had been receiving from my husband and neighbor was largely negative.

I wasn't yet comfortable with this new beau, when he proposed to me on Valentine's Day of 1983. He had purchased a ring of intent to a commitment as boyfriend and girlfriend...with the understanding he was serious about me; about all of us. He wanted to marry me right away but consented to my (ambivalence) desire to give this some time. He felt confident that he had me with this purchase and proposal. I felt he needed to slow down and take notes with time and experience as our guide, as to whether he would feel the same commitment from his initial proposal.

My new boyfriend was an only child from his father's second marriage. He had been raised by his father with a very conservative background. I had been his second serious relationship, and I didn't think he knew quite what he was getting himself into. He unfortunately met my next-door neighbor husband during our dating. My about to be ex-husband was very intentional and mean spirited in his efforts to dissuade my boyfriend, by expressing *his* opinion of *me* to him. My new boyfriend/fiancé took offense to everything this neighbor was sharing, which then turned into a scuffle (in front of our children and other neighbors) My soon-to-be ex-husband started a pathetic fist-to-cuff fight. I thought for sure, my fiancé would change his mind about wanting to court me any further, by running for the hills, but he didn't. The scuffle didn't change anything for him, except to prompt me to go through with the divorce my husband had filed nearly a year and a half prior.

While dating my future (second) husband, he proved to be very attentive to Kristina and her siblings. His attention to Kristina helped her thrive. Because she had been getting over heart surgery and other medical challenges during her short two years, she was not meeting all the benchmarks of children her age. She had much to accomplish from all that she endured. With this different and apparently nice man in our lives, Kristina was getting much-needed love and support from another positive, loving person in her life. As a result, Kristina started getting stronger, happier, and even learned to walk by the time we got married on December 31, 1983! By then, she had turned three years of age. Our lives seemed to turn the corner from desperately lost to hopefully found and desired.

Marriage, especially when it is your second, your new husband's first, comes with some hearty expectations and bumpy roads. It went from marital "bliss" to marital "blisters". Trying to blend two people, much less several relatives, into a healthy, thriving cohesive family unit is nearly impossible if one doesn't have the emotional intelligence or stamina that it takes to do so. My new husband and I were not married long, when the wheels on our bus started to turn square. In other words, we were plugging along. My husband wanted us to join his church, which we did. We were baptized as a family into the Episcopal Church.

We met a lot of people who seemed to love and support our new family, and so, we started socializing more at church functions. I joined the choir, and we joined a softball league. When it came to my husband's relationship with the kids, he and Kristina got along great, but he had high expectations and a short fuse for my other children. My two oldest would misbehave and not listen to his commands, often leaving him feeling very frustrated and ineffective as a father.

When he decided we weren't making enough money, he convinced me to find employment. At the time, Kristina was attending an Infant Stimulation/Early Intervention Program for half the day. I found part time employment with the San Diego School District as a "special education" aide. Trying to get off work on time, to be home when Kristina got off the bus, proved to be too much, and soon, I had to quit. After receiving a government grant, I started taking a couple of college classes, but I was always stressed out getting to Kristina's bus on time to pick her up, or make my classes on time or skip one altogether due to her illnesses. The scheduling thing caused a lot of tension between my new hubby and me. Then there was the financial burden, no thanks to my ex-husband's stubborn inability to pay child support on time or at all, as well as his refusal to accompany or assist me to any of Kristina's many medical appointments.

Unfortunately, up until I met my second husband, my family or my ex-husband's family, were barely supportive or available. They conveniently disappeared, missing in action, so to speak, from the time Kristina was born until I met him. I think they were frozen in thought, not knowing what to say, or how to care. I guess they believed it was better to let me figure things out rather than 'interfere'. I was very stubborn and thought I could handle everything on my own, especially since Mr. Right came along.

My husband was not responding well to me or my two kids. We were too chaotic for him. I think he finally realized that his expectations of being a positive, impactful stepdad and second husband, were not realistically being met. Much of the time we were married, he fumed silently, disappearing emotionally, until he would unexpectedly explode. This didn't go well with my children or me. In an attempt to restore peace in our home, we sought counseling from our church priest. We struggled for two and a half years in counseling before silently, privately giving up emotionally trying anymore.

Kristina's father and girlfriend seemed to back off with their troublemaking once I married Mr. Right. They finally moved about thirty minutes away and had less and less to do with us unless it was concerning child support. This was another angst my new husband always managed to be angry about — my ex-husband paying child support late or skipping payments. It seemed like every month this became another reason for my husband and I to argue…over money.

In the summer of 1986, my husband took us all on a road trip to Peoria, Illinois. That trip was the end-all-be-all —

the only trip we ever went on together. Our road trip ended up looking like something straight out of one of Chevy Chase's *National Lampoon* movies. Bags flying off the top of the car while driving down the freeway; kids getting dragged out of the car to get spanked on the side of the road; husband being placed in the hospital for a blood infection! I also found out I was pregnant (again), which would be my fourth child and his first.

While pregnant, I was advised to get an amniocentesis. To my relief, everything looked normal, and my husband was elated. (Even if the results came back not so positive, I wouldn't have done away with this pregnancy.) We had her on February 24, 1987. Now we had two babies, Kristina and then my youngest daughter. For at least a year, my husband seemed very happy being a father to his own child, but soon, we were right back to fighting, arguing over petty grievances. Whether it was what his step-kids did or didn't do, how I didn't do this or that, or how my kids were treating his newborn, nothing seemed to please him. I couldn't stand his silent treatment and anger, and in the back of my mind, that little voice of reason that I ignored before marrying this man, was haunting me again. I did not want to stay married to an angry man for the rest of my life. Nothing I or my kids tried to do, seemed to make him happy. Initially, before we married, he seemed on the surface, to be happy and secure. Turns out, he wasn't a happy person underneath his façade of contentment. Brewing secretly below his emotional surface was self-loathing and anger, which, by marrying us, only made things worse for him.

After celebrating our anniversary, the previous evening, we had just barely passed the five-year mark, I asked him for a divorce. He surprisingly agreed, saying he had wanted this too for quite some time too but was afraid to ask. UGH! I was so shocked by his confession, I just wanted to slap him right there and then, in the car we were sitting in at the end of our driveway when I asked him this. I did want to stay friends (even though I was angry at his confession) with him and stated so, for the sake of our daughter. After it was all said and done, the surprising thing I realized, is he hardly ever took my kids anywhere, including Kristina, after we separated and divorced. He mostly snubbed them as if they didn't exist, which made me believe he hadn't really cared about or for them all along. This was an additional stab in the heart for me. I thought he was going to be my "Knight", not realizing he possessed an Achilles heel, my kids and I unwittingly exposed and attacked on a daily basis during our marriage.

He remarried a couple of years later, and his new wife made things difficult between us, by being jealous and threatened by my presence. She told me that she wished she would have met and had a child with him first and not the other way around. My fourth child at eight years of age, was diagnosed with Type 1 diabetes which didn't show its ugly head during the amniocentesis. Regardless, my relationship with my second ex-husband only became more strained and distant after he remarried and our daughter's devastating diagnosis. Once again, Kristina, my kids, and I were left to go it alone, struggling with minimal support from church friends and back on public assistance once again.

~~~Chapter Seven~~~

I really got an education about educating all of my children, including Kristina throughout their school history. Hers, as well as theirs, were fraught with inconsistencies, mostly due to funding, quality of the educators and staff. There were very mission-minded educators that made a positive difference in their early educational life. However, there were very few remarkable teachers during middle school and high school years due to budget cuts and ever-changing staff and administrators.

As Kristina graduated from her Early Infant Stimulation Program (which she started at three years of age and ended at the age of five), I knew NOTHING about special needs children's educational rights or needs as students. What was told to parents at that time by school professionals was what we usually accepted as the unalterable truth.

Kristina started out having many services provided to her in order to give her the best shot at being a happy, fulfilled young person. From the time she started kindergarten all the way until she left for middle school, there seemed to be more one-on-one services readily available to her. She was hard of hearing, required vision services, and had speech and physical issues. She also was cognitively impaired. Therefore, she was supposed to be supported with an educational plan that would address all of her "special needs". I, and all other educational staff would have an IEP (Individual Education Plan) held once-a-year, meetings to discuss, plan, and implement her many goals for success. However, once she was placed in middle school, services started to dwindle. Instead of one-on-one speech therapy twice a week, sessions were whittled down to group sessions twice a week. Many of the services she received in her early years were to the point of being laughably nonexistent as she aged out of the school system.

    I was constantly patrolling her care and education at these schools. As the years rolled by and it came time for the once-a-year meeting (referred to as an IEP…Individual Education Plan), I was already primed from previous years meetings, that I needed to prepared to have a fight on my hands for something the school district was going to cut down or completely out of Kristina's yearly educational plan, not because they felt Kristina didn't need the services. It was to try and gain or maintain control over their special education budget by cutting services. One constantly hears on local news; the district is cutting "wasteful" spending. Never mind what any or all administrational staff were agreeing to be paid, which included numerous and generous pay increases!

Just to get her back to riding the bus, took me two years of fighting with the district. (She had been driven to school by bus when she was younger for her Infant Stimulation Program.) I was bound by Kristina's school schedule; I couldn't hold down a job or go to school without considering her schedule, which didn't include her getting sick from time to time. This schedule thing was impacting me and my family economically. These consequences, these facts are what I brought to prove my case to the district during the many meetings and letters I wrote.

Finally, the district relented, and she was back on the bus. This extended her day, giving me more freedom to attend college classes or tend to my other children's needs. I felt as though I was being a good advocate for my daughter despite what the district felt about me as her mother...being a squeaky wheel and troublemaking. One must be vigilant regarding services rendered to your special need's child. Because if you aren't there requiring accountability from the service providers, then they get away with taking shortcuts! Continuity, accountability and cooperation between you, the teacher and the administrators or specialists are key to your child's incremental success!

One such IEP meeting for Kristina at San Diego High was particularly interesting and contentious. A "speech therapist", when it was her turn to present her "plan" for the coming year as well as a review of the past year, went on and on, saying words while counting on her fingers (this was how she taught the kids supposedly to speak) She stated that she was collaborating with all of Kristina's other teachers on Kristina's IEP goals. The home economics teacher wasn't aware Kristina could even speak. At the meeting, Kristina replied to the speech therapist, and all the other teachers were stunned, surprised that Kristina could actually speak! They all were under the impression that she was non- verbal, as she rarely uttered a word in their classes. This made the speech pathologist look pretty stupid and not credible, as if she was making events up regarding collaboration and cooperation for Kristina's speech plan. They didn't even know the speech teacher existed for Kristina. I was livid. It was then after the meeting; I insisted my daughter have another speech pathologist/therapist!

Another remarkable incident from school happened when Kristina returned home with her hair falling out in clumps. She seemed unsettled, upset and tired that day. When it came time for dinner, she wolfed down her food like she hadn't eaten all day. This made me angry, and my Mama Bear instincts immediately kicked in. I called the school to get to the bottom of this issue, reporting to the administration what I had observed. I went a bit drastic and informed them, I was going to call the police and child protective services if I didn't get the proper answer asap!

Soon after, I was informed Kristina's original teacher, who was excellent at her job, was laid up with a back injury. No one from the school called, or wrote to any parents to inform them of this issue. I didn't learn about the constant change of substitute teachers that were in and out of this class, mostly on a daily basis until I called about my daughter's disturbing condition. I had no idea there was substitute after substitute for these children and that the class was going haywire! What a nightmare that must have been for all those students. The most important thing about special needs students in the educational setting is they need consistency (positive). To have a different person every day during a crucial time in their lives is upsetting to them. Positive consistency when they are just starting school is, in my mind, the key to a more successful, creative, and happy person later in life.

What I learned from these gaps or gaffs is. a parent must be vigilant, take notes, and stay on top of your child's education. It is also a good idea not to always "swallow" teachers' or administrations' explanations…or rather excuses…as to why something didn't get done, or why or why not your child is or isn't allowed to attend certain functions that 'regular' educated peers of theirs are allowed to attend, such as field trips, dances, proms and graduation. I made sure Kristina could do all and any of those events, even if that meant I had to go as a volunteer or chaperone! It's more than okay to disagree and ask questions. Have them repeat or explain further if you don't understand what was conveyed. Sometimes with the school system, there can be a lot of smoke and mirrors — meaning the administration can talk a good game, but the results speak for themselves. It is you who must keep watch over the differences and improvements your child is or isn't making. It is also you, who needs to duplicate the curriculum that is being taught to your child in the classroom at home as best you can.

Kristina graduated from high school in 1999 with her peers (actually, she received a certificate of completion) and continued with the school district's offer to continue to be educated under the district rules known as a "transition to work/learning" program until age twenty-two. After completing that program, there were many other accessible "day" programs for adult people with special needs, in order to continue to enhance, broaden, stimulate their minds with various activities. Depending on who *owns* these programs (licensed and funded by state/federal) is how in depth (or not) these activities can actually be. People with special needs, deserve to live out their lives just as equally importantly as their peers, by being able to have access to viable programs that assist in the ability to express these precious souls' individuality through work, creativity such as art, music, technology and physical fitness or well-being.

If your adult child lives at home with you, it is important to be alert to the changes your (adult) child may exhibit after they arrive home from whatever program they attend. For instance, my Kristina came home several times cold and hungry. I found out later, an employee, or job coach, was sleeping in the park with his/her clients in the car, while the clients listened to the job coach's choice of music rather than take them to a library, movies, or job site! Because the educational system does not pay these people very much, the care of your adult child with disabilities can unfortunately come at an extremely high price.

If you decide to place your child in a group home or community, which is where my daughter is currently living, then you being "in charge" is limited. As a parent, you have limited input at the "goals" meeting, but ultimately, the day-to-day nuances of your child is relinquished to the house manager or group home owner, leaving you mostly out of the loop. Since I don't have what's known as "conservancy" over my daughter, unless I ask or check up on her often enough, I am no longer privy to her daily living, much like when one's adult child (without disabilities) moves out or away from your home. I am still able to attend those once-a-year meetings to review and plan Kristina's past and future growth, which is nice, but not necessarily required, only one's desire.

Honestly, with Kristina (and other adults who have special needs), there usually aren't any drastic changes cognitively or health wise going on for her…for the better. That is not to say she didn't learn or is not thriving or benefiting from her adult environment. For me to expect her day program (Saint Madeline Sophie Center) to perform some miracle for Kristina to suddenly be more verbal through taking speech therapy classes, or more aware cognitively through taking other classes and community outings, would be setting myself up for constant disappointment. She pretty much is where she is currently is in all areas of her cognitive and physical life as an adult. The "needle of change" as far as forward movement or overall improvement for her, moves very, very slowly, if at all. I can only hope she is getting something good out her current day program and home placement, so that she is continually happy and healthy for as long as she is able.

    I, on occasion, used to fantasized or look at the preverbal "if only" kind of gander into the future, by thinking about the many things in the life my daughter will not be able to take part in...such as marrying, careers, having children, etc., like her siblings and other adult children are experiencing. I know all too well this kind of thinking is futile. Our "normal children" as adults, do not have life any easier either by having to deal with the daily grind of living and surviving this life, that we, they sometimes take for granted. Another perspective, one that is more productive and positive, is to look at things for Kristina; she'll be missing out on all the grief, heartaches, disappointments, etc., but has a completely different set of issues that come from being cognitively impaired.

~~~Chapter Eight~~~

By the time Kristina turned eight, I had divorced my second husband. Up until then, Kristina's health and education ebbed and flowed mostly better than expected under her previous circumstances. Life for her medically, educationally, and emotionally had normalized mostly when I married for the second time. Once I divorced however, she and I had faced other challenges that unexpectedly appeared. Her siblings wanted to live with their father or their school friends, not with me or Kristina. Our house was broken, divided. I had taken on a whole new way of life that wasn't pretty, which included people who I thought would help and understand Kristina and myself. That would prove to be farther from the truth. My kids, now older, hated me. My son started using drugs as did my eldest daughter. They skipped school and eventually dropped out, both through all of their own upheaval, living elsewhere.

Divorced twice and on my own, my family's life once again spiraled downward. I lost hope, focus, dignity, and finances as well as family unity, with consequences that still haunt me today. Out of selfishness and a lost sense of self-worth, ignoring the God inside me, I made very poor choices, largely in part to being off course. My moral compass was dysfunctional and I didn't see a purpose or a way out. My little family suffered as did I, of course. What stayed on course, though, was my love and care for Kristina. If it hadn't been for her presence in my life, I am sure I would have caved in and ended my dreadful current state of being. I almost didn't see a way out of the darkness, unless it was because I knew deep down, I had to stay present and here for Kristina. God had other plans for my life! He uses our mess — if we so choose, to view our experiences with this perspective — as a message of enlightenment and hope for others!

By this time, my children were older and more able (or willing) to be disagreeable and disrespecting. I had taught them, through my poor choices, how to treat me...poorly. I was able to care for my youngest from my second marriage, sharing custody with her father, and my Kristina, but soon, that unraveled when he remarried. Eventually, I was forced off welfare when my son turned eighteen. My eldest daughter wasn't in school either. While on public assistance, I had been attending college off and on for years, but I had to drop out to find work. Kristina was nineteen, and I had to make the difficult decision to place her in a board and care. Otherwise, we were going to be homeless. This threw me into nightmares (literally) about my past life in foster care, thinking and feeling like I had given up on her and my other children. Eventually, I found work with the San Diego School District, working with children with special needs. For the next seventeen years, I saw Kristina often while she was in her group home with other people with special needs. She always seemed happy to see me and equally as happy when she returned to her caregiver's home. I always hated leaving her. She never seemed to hold any type of grudge toward me when I would come to pick her up in the future. Luckily for her or me, she isn't capable of such thought or attitude and I think somehow, she knew I would always be there for her. I could never give up on her…or for that matter, on all my children.

    I took Kristina back to live with me in 2015 because I felt she wasn't thriving where she had been for the past seventeen years. It wasn't that she was being ill-treated really. I just felt she needed more to her life. The group home she had been in, was great in many respects for the first 10-15 years, but the owner got older and started having medical challenges. Her children, who had grown up around many of the clients she had for years, were moving away and creating their own lives, which meant the owner wasn't able to enlist their help as much. My adult child wasn't getting out into the community much while living in this group home (unless I took her to visit with me on weekends), I made the decision to take her back to live with me once again. It was a risky move on my part, but one I will, to my dying day, never regret!

    By making this serious decision, I was able, through a process of discovery, to find the day program Kristina currently attends. This program is specifically designed to stimulate the minds and spirits of people with special needs through the many activities they offer. This day program is called ***St. Madeline Sophie's Center***. From Kristina's attendance, I discovered another buried treasure. ***Noah Homes*** — a board and care facility who have selflessly cared for approximately ninety individuals with various disabilities for three decades. I placed my daughter on a waiting list. I vowed that I would not place Kristina into any other board and care group situation unless it was with Noah Homes. It took a total of two years after signing her up on that waiting list, but she finally was accepted in. I honestly think this was God's plan for her life all along. She is happy, thriving, loved and cared for by her peers and the people who give of their lives to care for these angelic souls!

~~~Chapter Nine~~~

Upon reflection of my experiences with Kristina and my other children, I can say, *Whew! We are still all accounted for!* If I could have had a crystal ball to see a much better way forward, would I have changed course? I am tempted to say yes, but that is just fantasy. If given the opportunity, perhaps I would have done quite a few things differently and conceivably better for me and all my children. I cannot continue to beat myself up for the past choices I made. That's much like trying to put spilled milk back in the container it came from before it got spilled. Impossible! I had lost sight of my purpose. In fact, through it all, I hadn't really realized what my purpose for being on this planet was. Most of the time, I "reacted" instead of "responded" thoughtfully, maturely, selflessly. I was angry, depressed, and literally wanted to give up so often than I can count on one hand. I think my children feel to this day, like I had given up on them, doing just the bare minimum. I can honestly and humbly admit, I would not be nominated for "Mother of the Year".

For the sake of argument or reflection, let's say I was

given the opportunity for a "do-over". These would be the things I would do better, faster, or not at all. Perhaps you can avoid making the same mistakes from my experiences.

I would perhaps do or not do the following:
- Prayed more, inviting my sense of a higher power or God into my life every day on a consistent basis, adding to my overall faith
- Joined more tribes or communities of parents who were also going through similar experiences as myself and my family
- Not allowed undeserving, undesirable people into my life, who didn't get or want to understand Kristina, her siblings or me for that matter
- Had journals to organize and preserve the experiences of doctor's visits, educational plans and issues, as well as personal, important bench marks of Kristina's progress
- Involved extended family by asking for more contact and assistance and interaction with Kristina
- Received more emotional support for myself through professionals and attend church more often instead of searching for answers and assistance from "friends" or potential partners
- Treated all my children to more one-on-one time as well as considered them all precious gifts and thinking and acting toward them as such

- Had more patience with myself and others, as well as forgiveness and compassion for others' willful ignorance

Since November of 2017, Kristina has been living with ninety other folks and their caretakers in an incredible community called **Noah Homes** located in Spring Valley, California. I see her as often as I liked (until Covid-19 hit however) and am involved with her day to day as much as I request or desire. This community of hardworking people, who care for adult children with special needs like my daughter, are to be congratulated and respected as heroes. Most do not do it for the pay, which is mostly minimum wage and maybe some benefits. It's their "calling" in life. They find meaningful purpose and joy working with our "angels" with different abilities.

Kristina's day program is called the **St. Madeline Sophie Center**. Located in El Cajon, California, this day program services approximately four hundred adults at various stages of ability and age. These precious souls are given the opportunity to express themselves through creative classes of art, music, dance, community service, etc. What is also offered is the opportunity and challenge, mastering daily life skills and goals that are manageable and measurable. They, with the guidance of a work coach, find meaningful employment out in the community and so much more. The attendees are treated with respect and dignity. Because of the existence of this program, my daughter is not languishing in some apathetic employee of another god awful "day program" in a cold car, listening to that person's choice of music or at some food court at a mall all day, wasting away from absolute boredom and indifference.

When Kristina comes to visit my home on weekends (before Covid-19 and hopefully soon after vaccinations take place for the residents and the public), I take in her laughter and moments of her sense of humor. I listen more, taking mental note of her joyful face, her nuances as a middle-aged person who still loves to be around her mother, yet, who also loves to be around her peers. She is a loving and gentle soul. Every one of her peers and caregivers love Kristina. My friends, whether at church or otherwise, love being around Kristina because she is so calming and charming. Though she is mostly nonverbal, her quiet personality says volumes. She speaks the language of unconditional love, and that is what others receive when they are around her. That is what I am most privileged to receive as well…gratefully.

I remember a time when people would just stare or make fun of Kristina (little children mostly). Now, with society's increased awareness of people with special needs, it is not so shocking or unusual to see them in various public settings such as schools, television, starring in movies, commercials, Special Olympics. The sky is the limit for people with special needs, of late, which in my mind is a win-win for everyone. Our general education population of kids get to experience people with different abilities more now than when I was a child. This is a GREAT thing for them and the child with a disability.

In the United States, people with disabilities, are not necessarily *put away* in institutions and hid from the public as if they are aliens, freaks, or shameful. We, as a society, are better off emotionally when we witness people with different abilities being given so many more opportunities to shine and thrive than say, fifty or more years ago. It is to be expected currently, that people born with special needs, especially children, will be able to live as "normal" a life as any other *normal* person or child, especially if given the privilege and resources to do so.

My (adult) child, Kristina, is doing just that. After almost forty years of witnessing her perseverance through many of her early medical challenges as well as her educational ups and downs, she and I get to witness her thriving and being happy today. I am so proud of her accomplishments and am privileged to say *I AM* her biggest fan... as just her mom!

I am reminded of all the things my family and I have been through in the past, is not without a purpose. I couldn't see this while in the middle of several chaotic moments. Many times, I thought my faith was being tested, my resilience was being tested, and that God had forgotten me. Far from the twisted truth that I allowed to fester in my mind and heart. I roamed around for solutions on my own power...at least forty years in the desert so to speak. I know now that faith in a higher power (God…for me) is purposeful for myself and others who may bond with the things that I have shared. We are here to lift each other's spirit and support each other to a higher more uplifting plane with actions of positivity and growth. My past pain has catapulted me into action at present, and these actions hopefully can speak to those who read this story I have shared.

~~~2020 Reflections & Analysis~~~

In this last chapter, it is my intention to look back to the past with forward thinking as to what is current and existing today. Hopefully, this will piece this story neatly together so that no one finishes this book wondering "what happened afterwards?" It's a way for my readers to see how everything in the past is reflected in this story today.

This story is not meant to give voice to a victim mentality. It might seem like that at first. I wrote chronologically to lead my readers into the forest and along the trail of how Kristina's life came to existence, and in my hindsight view, divinely set up.

I purposely left out the names of the those intimately involved to preserve the dignity and anonymity of each person. It also wasn't my goal to vilify anyone in my story. In my description of each character within the telling of this story, it may seem as though I am saying each possessed extraordinarily flaws. Being perfectly humble and honest, that is our human condition. We each have different amounts of broken or flawed pieces of ourselves. It is through the bravery and willingness to live each day, that will hopefully lead to wisdom and truth individually and societally, if we are so fortunate to witness and speak about it, resulting in positive change for ourselves and the world around us.

I have to say in this story, I was at the top of that list of imperfections. I take full responsibility for how I reacted...less than optimally, honest, or maturely to each person, place, or event. Thus, why I do not name individuals or get into "nitty-gritty" details any more than necessary. The person and story I tried to focus on was and is mainly about my daughter with Down syndrome, who I do name and do so, openly. I also have to admit that while things looked impossible or bleak when I was young, I finally realized here of late, that my set of circumstances from the past, was leading me forward, step by step, into my current purpose. If I had realized this sooner, I wouldn't have allowed guilt, shame or blame to hold me back from all God meant for me to be, do, have and share.

Chapters *One* **through** *Four*, my intention was to share how my husband and I met, our marital difficulties, the betrayals, giving birth to a child unexpectedly with Down syndrome at an early age of twenty-four, and how her birth and being a young single mother, left me shaken and further disrupted emotionally.

My husband and I were so "night and day" in our upbringing. My husband's family, I depicted as *Leave It to Beaver* or *Father Knows Best* — two television series characterizing times in the 50s and 60s as an ideal family dynamic. Though I didn't really know every intimate detail of my husband's family, what I observed and what he confided about his family at the time, seemed as I described.

I, on the other hand, had a *less than optimal* childhood, one of sexual, physical, and emotional abuse, which ultimately put me in four foster homes. It is through those experiences; I feel as though I was (and still am) more empathetic toward others but not necessarily affording that attitude towards myself. I tended to root for the "underdogs" of society, yet sadly and painfully broken all the while. I have had many therapy sessions or psychological assistance to help sort through the "trash" of my life. Where I am today, is a lot calmer, wiser, not so willing to create or be part of more chaos. I feel I am more spiritually grounded and want to be part of a societal solution by raising awareness where "underdogs" need uplifted, especially people living with special needs and their families.

My first husband, shortly after we divorced, married who he left me for and lived with his second wife for thirty years. He suffered from many facets of mental illness, which I only experienced the tip of the iceberg in the short time we were married. After his marriage to his girlfriend, he started displaying more manic depressive and bipolar behaviors, which his second wife dealt with for thirty years, as best she could with whatever "tools" she had within her. I wouldn't have been able to live long-term with him and his illnesses as she chose to. He ultimately took his life (though there is speculation that he was on so many different drugs for this diagnosis, that his death was accidental) in March of 2011. His children miss him, but they did back when he left us in 1980. However, now...there is a *permanence* to his departure. We all feel the unfortunate loss from his unnecessary death. He was such a smart man, possessing so much potential for everything electronics. He wanted to be a part of discovering bionic or robotic arms. I wish he had chosen college, but that was never to be. We as a couple, did manage to have moments of fun with each other. Just recently, while watching a movie, I remembered, he taught me how to play chess and the game "GO" while in our navy days, and he later did manage to apologize to me about how he had treated me so badly before his death.

    I have moved on, of course, and have grown to feel much compassion for him. I didn't recognize his behaviors toward me as having a mental illness. I internalized his behaviors as my fault. Many, later on, thought he had "lost it" and was "crazy". My husband did display bizarre behaviors (I thought it was only from excessive pot smoking really) while we were married. Military, medical doctors even categorized as him having such, while in the Navy, but this wasn't acted upon with therapeutics then and was not formally, correctly diagnosed until his second marriage. His behaviors became even more worrisome after we divorced. While being married to his second wife, he tried several times in different ways to kill himself, with S.W.A.T. called out at least two times.

As Kristina got older, she never called her father by his birth name because he didn't really see him that much. She didn't know him as a father figure. His second wife didn't like to acknowledge our existence, and in a way, I liked not seeing her. Today, I still feel that way as it would bring back old hurts. Though I have forgiven them both, it is easier to have the "out of sight, out of mind" mentality. His parents eventually passed away, but before doing so, his mother ended up suffering from dementia. The ironic and sad part of her decline toward the end of her life, she didn't remember who I was when her daughter brought her along to attend my 50th birthday party. Though that was a kind and beautiful moment to see her, it was also hard and sad to realize how much she didn't remember and witness her drastic decline while she attended this event.

My husband's sudden confession and departure left me and my children traumatized for years. That alone, sent my self-esteem spiraling down. Whilst giving birth to Kristina on the same day as his girlfriend's birthday, through the years, it was any wonder why my husband chose his girlfriend over my daughter. He hardly celebrated our daughter's birthday. He would make his girlfriend/wife bring presents to Kristina, hardly ever visiting Kristina. After Kristina became a teenager, this dwindled even more. His appearances for any of her doctor's appointments or hospital stays were next to nothing. I often wondered about the guilt he had to have felt for leaving us, for having a daughter like Kristina, and marrying a woman who insisted that he be with her always instead of with his daughter for birthdays and Christmas. I wondered if these things were the reasons why it sent him down some dark rabbit holes of shame and sorrow, magnifying his mental illnesses. He usually masked this by being aggressively hateful and uncooperative toward me for several years. His second wife might refute this, of course.

Having Kristina when and how I did was mind blowing and stressful. I was not prepared emotionally or financially and felt very inept as a mother (no thanks to my unresolved upbringing) of my other children, as a wife, and equally undeserving to be Kristina's mother. *Why did God choose me as her mother?* I thought. Some people would look at me and Kristina a lot when we were out in public often with pity. Some would even express sorrow for me and her, saying "I must be someone special" to have a child like her. I never felt *special*! Quite the opposite. I think now, looking back, there ***was*** a divine purpose throughout her life and mine.

Chapter *Five*, I felt I had a more developed a sense or intuition with regard to Kristina's health. I didn't realize I had this, except through my many experiences with Kristina and her army of doctors or specialists' appointments. I was so busy believing others perspective of me, that I often argued with my intuitions and made incorrect decisions. I was also thrust into a world I could have never imagined. In my already challenging childhood during the 50s/60s/70s, if there was someone who appeared to be "different", we as children/teenagers, behaved with such rancor or fear of "these" people who were different. Plus, there were hardly any involvement with people with disabilities because they weren't always in plain sight, mingling with "cognitively, physically *normal*" people. That was unheard of. Most were placed in "institutional" settings, out of sight of public view and scrutiny.

One such case or story of this that I personally know, was my best friend from my first high school. She told me horror stories of how her parents went through hell and back with her eldest brother who had special needs. They kept him at home in the beginning of his life, placed him, as he got older and more aggressive toward their mother, in an institution only to find out later that he had gotten severely beaten many times and even raped!

They rescued him out of that situation and took him home to live with them once again. Being that these parents were older, I am sure their lives weren't easy to deal with under those circumstances of that poor man's past traumas. He stayed with his parents until his passing in 2012. My friend says she would never regret his existence but acknowledges, his needs did seem to supersede theirs as a large family. However, she says, he taught her how to love and put her on a path to be an educator of people with special needs. She says that her brother and her still have "special" conversations through lots of prayer.

Since having Kristina at such an early age in the 1980's, it seemed as if it was an era by which, the beginning of awareness for society to properly support people with special needs started shifting for the better. People were struggling to fight for the rights and privileges for these people who couldn't necessarily advocate for themselves and didn't ask to be born with special needs, by slowly and steadily changing laws and actions financially, educationally, medically.

For the first 2-5 years, Kristina had so many different health issues suddenly appear out of nowhere, having so many different levels of care. More than half the time, I just *"winged it"* regarding helping her. Call it intuition, call it being a "helicopter mom", but I was in constant fear of doing something wrong or not enough for her. Kristina and I *both* despised going to any doctor out of fear and frustration, as most doctors were struggling with their own hidden biases and as it is said often in the medical field, doctors **practice** medicine, so it is not a perfected profession!

I literally had to FORCE her pediatrician by my insistence, to listen to me with regard to what I felt was a "failure to thrive" by going beyond his "expertise, directly instead to Kristina's heart specialist, who then (thankfully) supported my intuition by allowing a serious look into her heart to check out what might be contributing to her not thriving. Because of this action of Dr. Kishani, one of her many specialists, Kristina is alive today, and that part, at that time of her life, was critical and uplifting for me. Finding a rare, fatal heart condition made me believe in the power of my intuition and to always question the validity of medical professionals if one has an inner sense (not just a mental illness!) that things don't feel or seem quite right with a diagnosis! In other words, sometimes a second opinion is not only necessary, but within the rights of a patient or parent of a patient to have and do!

I have often felt (and stated) throughout this book, unprepared for having Kristina, and then dealing with all the other life altering things (divorce) that would follow, later after she arrived. I knew I had to do everything within my power to care and support her, but doing so mostly alone at such a young age, I lost my way, my energy and my focus which often waxed and waned. I wasn't always *ALL IN*. I felt my cup half full, would frequently run bone dry! Run out of patience, positivity, vision or spiritual faith for the future. I was constantly being barraged with challenging negativity from my first husband, his wife, from the welfare system, even doctors or educators.

I, many times, just couldn't keep it together. Not having the proper mechanisms to gain support from many professionals, albeit, social workers or therapists, I took pivotal opportunities for self-care in ways that weren't always in the best interest of all my children or myself really, which ultimately ended up negatively impacting or scaring most of my children. Many of my decisions were very worrisome. I learned everything the hard way and others, like my children or perspective partners, suffered. If I could take it all back, I'd be tempted to tweak some of the things I did wrong with regard to my responses and actions or lack of action. But life is not a board game like chess, to play over and over again, hoping to finally get good enough to master the game.

Chapter *Six*, I was three years older, feeling old and washed up, going through the medical nightmares with Kristina as well as trying to raise her siblings. My next-door neighbor situation, fighting with my estranged husband still existed, when my future husband walked into my life. At the time, I called this man my *knight in shining armor*. Once we started dating, all hell broke loose with the about to be ex-husband who still lived next door to me. They got into a pathetic fist fight over petty man stuff. I think my soon-to-be ex-husband wanted to negatively impact this new guy's perspective about dating me further. This didn't deter my current boyfriend's desire to continue, but later on when we finally married, my ex's behavior with child support and custody proved to be too much for my new husband to handle. I, was too much for him to handle! He had very high idealistic, expectations that frustrated him on many emotional levels. The pressure on my new husband to provide for kids that weren't his, was greater than he had anticipated. Having Kristina wasn't necessarily a problem for him, as he seemed to bond with her easily. But, by the time he came into my family scene, Kristina was outgrowing some of her health issues and was very responsive to my new husband and his family's attention. She thrived, started walking, and grew happier because of him. Because of the personality and expectation differences that existed between my new husband and I, filled with constant strife and arguments, our marriage lasted a total of five years. Honestly, after six months, I started to see an emotional shift from him. It's not to say I thought him to be a bad person or father to my children or his...he wasn't. He became busy and emotionally unavailable, which worsened over time. The more he emotionally disappeared, the more I chased him in fear of losing him. Ultimately, with our irreconcilable differences, I did, and my kids lost what could have been a great father figure for them. He hardly ever looked back. He also didn't think I was headed in the "right" direction after he and I divorced. He didn't want or desire the drama and chaos I involved myself in later. He, being an only child growing up, desired a less dramatic and quieter way of living his life. He rarely offered to take any of my children from my first marriage, much less Kristina. He, after all, during our marriage, had his own child to bond with after we divorced. We managed to share responsibility in raising our child outside our marriage, who, at eight years of age, was diagnosed with Type 1 diabetes. I wanted a friendship, which proved too much for his second wife. I would attend various functions our daughter had from school or outside interests.

It became rare if we shared a Christmas together or celebrate Kristina's birthday. We both attended and witnessed our womanly child get married five years or so ago (I've lost track). We now have grandchildren together, which at various times of the year, like holidays, we dutifully get together in a strange and polite to show support and unity for our child and her children. That's family...the normal American way of life now!

Chapter *Seven*...the education system for all my children was one thing, but when it came to Kristina's education, it was another... filled with constant changes, more so than just 'regular education'. What a school district will or will not do, comes down to the bottom line of financing and possibly finessing or coalescing of faculty and staff. What funding that is available or not, to offer services needed for all the different types of disabilities or not. Money tied up for people/children with disabilities from state, local and federal institutions, seem always last up for debate. The changes can spin one's head and be very discouraging. It seemed at first, when Kristina entered the public-school system, their attention to every detail of Kristina's disabilities were right on point. She received the needed services for her cognitive functioning, speech, hearing, vision, and adaptive physical education. The older she became, the more those services were less available. It was not because the need was no longer there, but because of their burgeoning budgets. That is why, when it comes time to vote, it is important to research a certain candidate's stance on people with special needs whether they will support and fund full inclusion in the classroom or full benefits from Social Security, which includes medical access and care along with other services that are much needed support. More than half the time she was in the educational system, I spent advocating or fighting for Kristina's rights regarding her specific needs in education. Humans with disabilities (and seniors really) get the short end of the stick many times in any political arena.

VOTE for the candidates that actually DO make a difference in this area. Schools and other programs that support the needs of people with special needs are always scrambling for supportive funds because those funds are always on the chopping block with legislators. This is NOT right! People with special needs or preexisting conditions, need to live, as best they can, with as much creative possibilities, hopes and dreams, like any other human expecting, planning and implementing the ability to reach their highest potential in their own lives. People with disabilities, need continued support in order to be able to live in dignity, not poverty and barely getting by.

Being your child's advocate and parent, as they grow, will take not only your emotional and physical support, but your financial support. Be politically aware of the laws that will affect their future. Many times, after your child grows out of some of the frightening health issues from their infancy, there will be life things that will appear, like continued educational and therapeutic needs, dental, vision and other hospital or medical needs as they age.

Another thing to consider is YOU. What will you do when this child becomes an adult? What will your needs be? Will there be family member to take over if something happens to you? What home environment will best suit their needs? These topics need to be considered and discussed always, because one never knows when the "light switch" to our own lives will be shut off permanently (especially during this pandemic and any in the future!). There is planning you need to consider and communicate, with others in your life of importance, which if started early enough while your child is young is time well spent. Even if these conversations or thoughts are just explored as inquiry or conversation with people in the know, then nothing discussed or planned. It's a seed planted! It's better than having that *unthinkable thing* happen, impacting your child's future negatively. It is very crucially important for you as the parent(s) of a child with Down syndrome (or other disability) to stay connected to resources offered through local, state, and federal assistance and programs. Social Security services, offers financial support for your child and their disability if there is a need for said support. It may be contingent on how much the whole household earns or brings in, as to whether financial support will be given. There may be services offered through the state where you reside, that could greatly assist in pointing parents toward provisions of financial assistance in order to receive various specialty care services, such as dental, vision, speech, etc. Stay connected and join other groups that offer support through parental peer participation…like "meet-ups" to further your child's future positively and to gain more knowledge for your situation. Having other parents who are going through basically the same things you are, can be great support in the exchange of ideas and lifelong friendships!

Going forward, there is always the internet, to check on various facets of your child, but be mindful; do your due diligence. Remember to verify what you have read and make sure that the information is from reliable sources. Try to resist believing everything, especially medical diagnoses. Call your doctor whenever you are confused or concerned. There is the library for resources as well, of course. Since I didn't have that extra edge of having the internet during the 1980s, raising a child with Down syndrome (or any other disability) today, having information readily available at your fingertips, seems easier but still daunting. This is why reaching out to peer groups in your area can be very helpful and never underestimated (even if it is on Zoom for now, due to Covid-19!). I don't claim in this book, to be a guru or have mastered anything significant in my life, especially when it comes to raising a child with special needs, just a person who has been around the block, knows a thing or two and could possibly help you think about things that perhaps, you haven't thought of before. I humbly acknowledge, I have a lot to learn and a long way to go to get there, God willing!

RESOURCES, ORGANIZATIONS & CONTACTS

I can be reached for any sharing, comments, advice, and questions. Please contact me at **kedsop1@yahoo.com**

There are also the following online resources, such as:

USAGOV Disability Services – They help in all kinds of areas of programs, funding information, and resources on the state and local level.

National Down Syndrome Society (NDSS) – They work with more than 375 affiliates, in addition to having support group meetings. Affiliates offer a wide range of programs and services for families of individuals with D.S.

www.dsdiagnosisnetwork.org (DSDN) – Connects new parents who just received the news that their baby has D.S. with support and information.

www.ds-health.com/lists – A compilation of D.S. email lists, newsgroups, and bulletin boards compiled by Dr. Len Leshin.

www.siblingssupport.org – A national effort dedicated to the concerns of the siblings of the child with special needs.

https://www.nads.org NADS, the oldest organization in the country serving individuals with Down syndrome and their families. It was founded in Chicago in 1961 by parents who chose to go against medical advice and raised their children with Down syndrome at home.

www.p2pusa.org – Provides emotional and informational support for families of children with special needs by matching parents seeking support with a trained support parent.

There are plenty of interesting books to read on the subject of Down Syndrome, as well as a recent, fascinating article "The Last Children Of Down Syndrome, published in a magazine called *The Atlantic* written December 2020. Many books written by other parents or sibling authors, share uplifting, encouraging, supportive stories for the purpose of enlightening professionals, parents and siblings.

About the Author

Karen Elaine Donahue, originally born in Waterbury Connecticut during the '50's, moved with her mother and siblings to Los Angeles County in June of 1967. She considers herself an "imported native", a Connecticut Yankee, in California, as a longtime friend described her as!

Currently residing in San Diego California, Karen has been blessed with the birth and lives of four children, seven grandchildren as well as being a great-grandmother!

She is and has been very active in the Episcopal Church since 1984 and currently is a member of Christ the King Episcopal church in Alpine, California. Before the pandemic, Karen had been a member of this church's choir as well as being a cantor and soloist at many other churches and choirs throughout San Diego for many years. She also sang for eight years consecutively, for the San Diego Padres national baseball team, our nations' National Anthem and various other public venues of note.

She has had the proud honor and privilege of accomplishing seven important fundraisers for HIV/Aids, that included riding a bike from San Francisco to Los Angeles and raising over $20,000 and riding over 2,500 miles (that's not counting the training rides either!)

She has accomplished many things in her life including surviving child abuse of many facets, poor foster home placements, and unfortunately, two failed marriages. She credits that traverse and survival to her deep faith with what she considers, her Savior Jesus Christ.

Currently because of her experiences with Kristina, working for the San Diego City School District for seventeen years, she is a passionate advocate for her daughter and people with special needs. They, her daughter, and the students she was privileged to work with, opened her eyes and consciousness to a whole new world of possibilities. She knows these experiences were her good fortune, in order to make a positive impact on these beautiful souls we all are graced by with their angelic presence in our lives and in society.

www.ingramcontent.com/pod-product-compliance
Lightning Source LLC
Chambersburg PA
CBHW031426290426
44110CB00011B/539